SKY SAILORS

DAVID L. BRISTOW

SKY SAILORS

TRUE STORIES OF THE BALLOON ERA

FARRAR STRAUS GIROUX
NEW YORK

Frontispiece: German balloonist Oscar Erbslöh, who won the 1907
Gordon Bennett Cup, an international gas balloon race, by flying 872 miles
from St. Louis, Missouri, to Bradley Beach, New Jersey.
He died in an airship accident in 1910.
Page 124: The crew of the French balloon Zenith *saw*
a lunar halo and luminescent cross during a night flight in 1875

Copyright © 2010 by David L. Bristow
All rights reserved
Distributed in Canada by D&M Publishers, Inc.
Printed in June 2010 in China by Toppan Leefung Printing Ltd.,
Dongguan City, Guangdong Province
Designed by Jay Colvin
First edition, 2010

1   3   5   7   9   10   8   6   4   2

www.fsgkidsbooks.com

Library of Congress Cataloging-in-Publication Data
Bristow, David (David L.).
    Sky sailors : true stories of the balloon era / David L. Bristow. — 1st ed.
        p.   cm.
    ISBN: 978-0-374-37014-5
    1. Balloonists—History—Juvenile literature.   2. Balloonists—Biography—Juvenile
literature.   I. Title.

TL616.B75 2010
910.4'22

2009037285

Dedicated to my parents, Ray and Doris Bristow. For Mom, and in memory of Dad.

CONTENTS

SKY SAILORS

In 1874, fishermen rescued a French couple who went down in the North Sea off the English coast. Le Tricolore *flew on many miles after its owners abandoned it*

INTRODUCTION

I N October 2009, I was putting the finishing touches on this manuscript when I heard the news that a six-year-old boy was flying alone above Colorado in his father's homemade balloon. The story quickly proved to be a hoax, but for a few glorious hours it seemed like a storybook come to life. At least that's how I saw it. Who wouldn't want to go sailing off like that, to ride the clouds and come down a conquering six-year-old hero, the envy of all your friends?

But that isn't just storybook stuff. Such a thing really happened. Back in 1858, two children in Illinois, ages eight and three, went up in a balloon by accident. They flew most of the night, rising perhaps four miles or more above the earth. Theirs is one of the true stories told here.

This is a book about the early years of human flight, from 1783 to the early 1900s. For more than a century before airplanes were invented, people explored the sky in balloons.

During that era, even airships were mostly still in the future. Airships are similar to balloons, except they have steering mechanisms and some form of propulsion that gives them the power to fly against the wind. For many years, balloonists tried improving their craft with all kinds of rudders,

sails, engines, and propellers. But no one built truly practical airships until the early twentieth century. They appeared about the same time as the first powered airplanes.

In the meantime, balloonists went wherever the wind took them. They told a doubting public it was a safe way to travel.

And it *could* be safe, as long as you didn't do certain dangerous things—such as fly in high winds . . . or into storm clouds . . . or over large bodies of water . . . or while lighting fireworks . . . or with only a trapeze to hang on to . . . or over an army that wants to shoot you down . . . or into the upper atmosphere where there's not enough oxygen to breathe . . . or over the Arctic ice toward the North Pole.

The men and women in this book did all these things. Most of them lived to tell about it.

Opposite: In 1824, an Englishman named Thomas Harris died when a faulty valve sent his balloon plummeting to earth. Some say he leaped from the basket to lighten the load so that his lady friend might survive the landing. She did, but whether Harris really jumped or was simply killed in the crash is unknown

The villagers of Gonesse, France, attacked the world's first hydrogen balloon in 1783. They thought it was a monster

THE BLACK MOON

THE FIRST BALLOON FLIGHTS (FRANCE, 1783)

STRANGE CREATURES lurk in the dark corners of the world, and sometimes they come out to get you. Countless stories tell it that way. On August 27, 1783, the villagers of Gonesse, France, saw the stories come true.

What they saw was round and silhouetted against the clouds. Some thought it was the moon, turned black and sinking to earth. Was it a sign of the Judgment Day foretold in the Bible?

The object sank to earth and lay on the ground. It wasn't the moon at all. It was about twelve feet across, and writhed like a living thing.

The people were terrified, but brave. Instead of running away, they attacked. They threw stones, beat the monster with flails, stabbed it with pitchforks. When they thought it was dead, they tied it to a horse's tail. The frightened horse dragged it across a field. The monster was never seen again.

Before long, everyone knew that the "monster" was really an unmanned balloon launched from Paris—just ten miles away. Parisians laughed about it, but the villagers had only acted on what they knew. How were they to know that the writhing object was merely a burst balloon venting hydrogen? No one had told them about it. They didn't even know such a thing could exist.

And just a few months earlier, no one else did either.

The French government soon issued a proclamation to the whole country: *Warning to the People on Kidnapping Air-Balloons.* It described the invention of the balloon and told people not to be frightened if they saw a "black moon" in the sky. It wasn't the end of the world. It was only a cloth bag filled with gas.

But that cloth bag filled with gas was the most exciting invention of its day. It meant that people would soon be able to fly. In a world of horses and sailing ships, that seemed like a miracle.

And it all started with a curious man and a simple idea.

JOSEPH THE DREAMER

PEOPLE FIGURED JOSEPH MONTGOLFIER would never amount to anything.

It wasn't for lack of opportunity. Joseph was the son of a wealthy papermaker. He could go to school and work for the family business. He just chose not to.

Joseph grew up in the small town of Annonay in southern France. He was bright, but didn't like school. As a teenager, he ran away from home. As an adult, he tried starting his own businesses, but failed every time.

His younger brother Étienne was different. Étienne was steady, worked hard, and studied to become an architect. And though he was next to youngest of the sixteen Montgolfier children, he was the one who took over the family business when their father retired. The business prospered.

But it was Joseph who had the idea that would change their lives.

The idea was so simple that anyone could have thought of it. Some say Joseph got this idea when his shirt was drying near the fire and began to rise. A better explanation is this: Joseph hadn't been much of a student, but now he loved reading science books and doing his own experiments. He studied how air expanded when he heated it. Everyone knew that hot air rises (such as smoke up a chimney). But Joseph found that when he filled a cloth bag with hot air, the bag also rose—and the bigger the bag, the more power it had to lift anything attached to it.

When he saw what Joseph was doing, Étienne became interested. The two brothers began working together on what they called a *ballon*. (A ballon, or balloon, is a round laboratory flask; it's also the French word for ball.) They built and tested a series of unmanned balloons, each one larger than the last.

Their method was to suspend the balloon over a fire pit. When the balloon was full, the brothers released it. Then it rose into the sky, sinking as the air inside it cooled.

On June 5, 1783, their first public launch in Annonay created a national sensation. It was a simple and beautiful idea to fulfill the ancient dream of flight.

However, Joseph and Étienne soon had a rival. His name was Jacques Alexandre César Charles, and he was not interested in hot air. His team built a balloon filled with hydrogen, a newly discovered gas that is lighter than air without being heated. It was Charles's balloon that the villagers of Gonesse mistook for a monster.

Both balloon teams had a new goal in mind. They wanted to build something large enough to carry people.

But would the king allow it?

Failed student, teenage runaway, and an all-around dreamer, Joseph Montgolfier went on to design and build the first balloon known to carry humans

ANIMALS IN THE SKY

A SHEEP, A ROOSTER, AND A DUCK—that's what the king agreed to. The Montgolfiers wanted to send a man up in a balloon (any man but themselves), but the king wouldn't hear of it. It was too dangerous.

Animals, not people, would be the first air passengers.

Maybe a balloon with passengers would come down too fast. Maybe land creatures couldn't even survive flight. Maybe there wasn't enough air to breathe. People had climbed mountains before, but was that really the same as leaving the ground?

There was only one way to find out.

And something else remained unclear. Joseph knew that hot air worked, but he still didn't quite understand why. He thought the fire changed the air into another kind of gas. He reasoned that burning different fuels created different kinds of gas.

His fuel choices got pretty strange. Back home in Annonay, he thought damp straw and chopped wool made the best balloon-filling fire. But after he and Étienne came to Paris, they began to gather old shoes and rotten meat to throw in as well.

They didn't realize that it didn't matter what they burned, as long as it heated the air. As it was, their smoky fire had only one advantage: it smelled so bad that it kept the crowds a safe distance away.

And on September 19, the crowd numbered in the tens of thousands. The flight was held at Versailles, southwest of Paris, to be near the royal palace. Everyone cheered as the three animals went up in a wicker cage tied to the balloon. In an eight-minute flight, they rose 1,700 feet before landing in a forest two miles away.

People came running. First on the scene was a young scientist named Jean-François Pilâtre de Rozier. He was relieved to find the animals alive. Now the king would surely allow people to fly—and Rozier was determined to be the first.

THE SECRET OF LIGHTER-THAN-AIR FLIGHT

THAT FALL, the Montgolfier brothers built their largest balloon yet. It stood about 75 feet tall and weighed 1,600 pounds. Painted blue and decorated in gold, it looked like an oversized ornament from the royal palace.

This balloon was different from the others in one important way: it would carry its own fire. A fire-basket made of wire hung below the balloon's open neck. Around this was a donut-shaped wicker gallery, where passengers would stand and feed the fire. The balloon would stay aloft as long as its fuel held out.

But how does a balloon work, anyway? We've already seen that even Joseph Montgolfier was a little fuzzy in his understanding of the subject.

Put simply, hot air lifts a balloon because it weighs less than cold air.

We don't usually think about air having weight, but it must—if it didn't, it would all just float away into space. The reason warm air rises has to do with buoyancy. Understand buoyancy, and you'll understand both how balloons fly and how boats float.

Think about a small rock and a large ship. You throw the rock into the water, and it sinks. The ship is much heavier than the rock, but it floats. Why?

A Greek mathematician named Archimedes figured this out in the third century B.C. The difference is density. The ship is big, but not dense. Though parts of it are dense (the anchor, for instance), a ship is mostly hollow. Water is denser than a ship, and a rock is denser than water.

So the big, heavy ship weighs *less* than the water it displaces. That's why it floats and the rock doesn't.

That, said Archimedes, is buoyancy. It's the upward force that keeps things afloat in a fluid.

Hot air rises for the same reason. Air is just a lot of floating molecules

Before he became the first balloon pilot, Rozier used to entertain his friends by inhaling hydrogen and setting it on fire as he exhaled

(tiny particles) of different gases. When the air is hot, the molecules get farther apart from each other. Thus, hot air is less dense (and less heavy) than cold air.

ROZIER'S QUEST

ROZIER GOT HIS WISH. He became the first balloon pilot (or *aeronaut*, as they would soon be called). The twenty-six-year-old had already made a name for himself as a scientist and inventor in his own right. He invented a breathing apparatus—sort of an early gas mask—to help workers in sewers. He founded a science museum, gave lectures, and entertained his friends by inhaling hydrogen and setting it on fire as he exhaled. The Montgolfiers were happy to let him fly their new balloon.

Rozier went up for the first time on October 15, 1783. He rose about 80 feet, with the balloon still tied to the ground. He made a series of these tethered ascensions, always going a little higher. With practice, he learned how to control the balloon's rise and fall by adding fuel or by letting the fire die down.

Fortunately for him, the Montgolfiers had apparently given up on old shoes and rotten meat. Rozier burned straw and alcohol-soaked rags. (He might have needed his gas mask otherwise.) After going as high as 300 feet, he was eager to cut the rope and go for a real flight.

That's when he received news he could hardly believe. The king still thought a cross-country flight was too dangerous. He wanted to send up two criminals sentenced to death. If they died, justice would be served. If they lived, they could go free.

"What?" Rozier said. "Allow two vile criminals to have the first glory of rising into the sky! No, no—that will never do!"

He talked to everyone he knew who might be able to sway the king. Finally a nobleman, the Marquis d'Arlandes, agreed to talk to the king.

In return, Rozier agreed to let d'Arlandes come along on the balloon flight.

So, with the king's reluctant permission, the two men climbed aboard the balloon on November 21. Many among the vast crowd probably thought the men were going to their deaths. It still seemed impossible that people could fly.

In fact, fire was probably their greatest danger. If the balloon fabric caught fire while they were in flight, the men could be in serious trouble. With this in mind, they brought along a bucket of water and one sponge apiece.

SOME FIRE, MY DEAR FRIEND!

THAT AFTERNOON, the ornate balloon again rose slowly into the sky—at last, without a rope. Now Rozier and d'Arlandes would go wherever the wind took them. They tended the fire-basket from opposite sides, about fifteen feet from each other.

The crowd stared up at the balloon, and d'Arlandes stared back at the crowd. They stood still and silent. It was an important moment in history and everyone knew it.

Only Rozier had no time for it.

"You are doing nothing," he said, "and the balloon is scarcely rising a fathom!"

D'Arlandes threw on a bundle of straw and stirred the fire. But soon he was distracted again. They were flying along the Seine River, and d'Arlandes began excitedly calling out names of places he recognized:

"Passy! Saint-Germain! Saint-Denis! Sèvres!"

"If you look at the river in that fashion, you will likely bathe in it soon," Rozier called to him. "Some fire, my dear friend, some fire!"

Soon the men had something else to worry about. Something made a loud pop, then another. It sounded like ropes breaking. Then d'Arlandes found a spot on the balloon that was full of holes where the fabric was burning.

"We must descend!" he cried, blotting the flames with his sponge.

"We are upon Paris," Rozier warned.

Though they'd launched the balloon outside the city, now they were above it. Landing among all the buildings and chimneys would be risky.

They inspected the balloon. To their relief, only two ropes had broken and the fabric fires were soon out. But by then they were sinking to rooftop level. Stoking the fire, they rose out of danger. At last, five miles and twenty-five minutes from their starting point, they landed safely in the country.

So ended the first (confirmed) human flight. But already, another was in the works. Professor Charles and his team were building a big hydrogen balloon for their own aerial journey.

The first balloon flight: Rozier and d'Arlandes fly along the Seine River in Paris

THE DAY OF TWO SUNSETS

BEFORE PEOPLE CALLED HIM "PROFESSOR," Jacques Alexandre César Charles was a clerk in the finance ministry. It was a promising career, but he left it after reading Benjamin Franklin's book *Experiments and Observations on Electricity*. After that, he wanted only to be a scientist.

Now it was time to risk his life for science. The Montgolfiers had shown that human flight was possible, but Charles's new balloon, *La Charlière,* was different from theirs in many ways.

There was the hydrogen, of course, which was difficult to make (more about that in the next chapter). But this balloon also had to be controlled differently. Hydrogen burns, so there could be no fire. To go higher, Charles would carry sandbags to throw out. To come down, he built a trapdoor valve at the top of the balloon. All he had to do was pull a rope to release some hydrogen.

On December 1, what may have been the largest crowd yet for a balloon ascension gathered to watch the flight. *La Charlière* was round and only twenty-seven and a half feet in diameter. Its silk panels were cut in red and yellow stripes that tapered at the top and bottom like wedges of an orange. Below, its chariot-like basket was tied to a large net covering the balloon's top half. This was to distribute the weight evenly so the balloon wouldn't tear.

Jacques Alexandre César Charles wanted to be a scientist like Benjamin Franklin. He designed and piloted the first hydrogen balloon

But if anyone thought that Charles and the Montgolfier brothers were enemies and not just rivals, Charles proved otherwise. He'd made a small balloon that he planned to release first. It would show the direction and speed of the wind above. As the crowd watched, he brought the emerald green balloon to Joseph Montgolfier. Handing him the string, he said, "It is for you, monsieur, to show us the way to the sky."

Before a huge crowd in Paris, Charles's balloon rose quickly into the sky, while the two pilots waved flags

Joseph released the balloon and the two men watched as it floated away to the northeast.

Then Charles and another man climbed into the basket. When a cannon fired to signal the launch, they rose into the air.

La Charlière proved more nimble than the Montgolfier balloon. It shot quickly into the sky while the aeronauts waved flags. The crowd let out a tremendous cheer.

Then the balloon sailed away, coming down 27 miles from its starting point. Peasants spotted the balloon as it flew lower and lower over the countryside . . . but fortunately the royal proclamation had worked. The country people were as excited as the city people had been. They chased the balloon, Charles wrote, "like children pursuing a butterfly."

The sun had just set when the balloon touched down, but Charles wanted to fly some more. He decided to go up alone. Without the weight of the other man, the balloon rose quickly—so quickly, in fact, that Charles rose higher than he intended.

From his heightened viewpoint, the sun popped up over the horizon again, and Charles was delighted to watch it set a second time. Surely, he thought, no one had ever seen two sunsets in one day.

But as he rose, the air grew thin and cold. He looked at his barometer. Based on the air pressure, he calculated that he was about 10,000 feet above sea level.

On only the third confirmed flight in history, Charles had risen nearly two miles above the earth. Suddenly he felt a sharp pain in his ears and jaw. He decided not to press his luck. He opened the valve and came down.

THE SECRET OF AVOIDING DEATH

CHARLES LANDED GENTLY IN THE FADING TWILIGHT. For reasons known only to himself, he never flew again. He would devote the rest of his life to scientific research, not adventure.

It went differently with Rozier. Less than two years later, the first man to fly a balloon became the first to die in one. He tried to cross the English Channel in a double balloon, with separate chambers for hydrogen and hot air. The balloon caught fire and Rozier crashed to his death. He was mourned as a fallen hero.

All the original balloon men were regarded as heroes. And though some people thought the invention useless, others felt that a new age had begun. They even talked of flying to the moon.

The story is told of an old man who watched Charles's flight from a window. His friends had to make him watch—he said he didn't believe in this balloon nonsense. But as Charles rose into the sky, the old man fell to his knees, crying.

When his friends asked why he wept, he said, "They will find out the secret of avoiding death, but it will be after I am gone!"

Because now that people could fly, anything was possible. *Anything*.

MORT DE MME BLANCHARD (1819)

The death of Sophie Blanchard, part of a series of balloon collecting cards printed in Paris between 1890 and 1900

QUEEN OF THE NIGHT SKY

SOPHIE AND JEAN-PIERRE BLANCHARD (FRANCE, 1784–1819)

JEAN-PIERRE BLANCHARD was injured and unconscious but still alive. He had been flying for the king of Holland at the royal castle when suddenly his hot air balloon plummeted from 65 feet.

The fifty-five-year-old had suffered a stroke. Lying helpless in his balloon basket, he was unable to throw straw on the fire. The hot air cooled quickly. The balloon fell and the basket struck hard.

Onlookers rushed forward to find him entangled in ropes and balloon fabric. He wasn't moving.

Some sources say Blanchard woke up later that day. Others say he was still comatose when he was taken home to Paris a few days later. Either way, he was never the same and only lived a few more months.

Blanchard had once been France's premier balloonist, but his career had faded over the years. Now he was dying and deeply in debt. His wife, Sophie, cared for him night and day, and he worried about what would become of her.

"My poor dear," he told Sophie, "when I am dead I fear you will have no other recourse than to throw yourself into the water."

Jean-Pierre Blanchard died on March 9, 1809. He didn't live to see how badly he'd underestimated his wife. He had forgotten one important thing:

She knew how to fly balloons, too.

YOUNG JEAN-PIERRE

JEAN-PIERRE'S STORY begins when he was twelve years old and built his first invention, a rattrap. When he was sixteen he built a velocipede, an ancestor of the bicycle. Though he never had much schooling, he was good with mechanical things.

And he dreamed of flying. In 1781, two years before the balloon craze began, he built a flying machine based on his study of bird flight. It had four flapping wings powered by the pilot's arms and legs. It probably never left the ground, but some said Blanchard flew it 80 feet in the air.

He probably spread the story himself. Jean-Pierre liked to talk about himself, not always truthfully.

He made another boast soon after the invention of the balloon. He promised to end the rivalry between Charles and the Montgolfiers by outdoing them all. Soon he was building balloons with oar-like wings in hopes of flying against the wind.

In time, Jean-Pierre toured Europe and America as the world's first professional balloonist—flying at special events for a fee, or launching his balloon from within a fenced-off enclosure and charging admission. He was also first to demonstrate the parachute . . . but he didn't try it himself.

He used his dog instead. Though the dog probably never did anything to deserve it, Jean-Pierre placed him in a little basket attached to a parachute, then dropped him from 6,500 feet.

Instead of falling, the parachute caught a rising air current and carried the dog up into the clouds. Jean-Pierre's balloon rose, too. They saw each other somewhere above the clouds, and the dog barked with joy.

But again the wind separated them. The parachute came down after Jean-Pierre had already landed. The dog was unhurt. Being a dog, he probably forgave his master—at least the first time.

Many humans were less tolerant of the prickly aeronaut. A modern historian named L.T.C. Rolt called Blanchard "a ruthless egotist, a mean-spirited and jealous man . . . who begrudged others the smallest share of the limelight."

But there was something about him: even people who disliked Jean-Pierre admired his courage. And he needed plenty of that on the flight that made him famous.

CROSSING THE ENGLISH CHANNEL

Only twenty-one miles of sea separate Dover, England, from the northern coast of France. The Strait of Dover is the narrowest part of the English Channel, which divides the British Isles from the European continent. As seas go, it isn't large.

But try crossing it in something as fragile as a balloon. Suddenly it looks big and dangerous. Between the white cliffs of Dover and the rocky French coast lie nothing but cold, gray waves. If your balloon goes down, you'll probably drown or die of exposure before a ship finds you.

Blanchard decided to fly the Channel in 1784, just a year after the first balloon flights. Though he'd flown only a few times himself, he was eager to do what no one had done. All he needed was money for a proper balloon.

That's when he met John Jeffries, an American doctor living in England. Jeffries had money to spare, and wanted badly to go on a balloon voyage. He and Blanchard struck a bargain: Jeffries would pay for the balloon; Blanchard would let the doctor ride along.

It was not a happy partnership. Blanchard eagerly spent Jeffries's

Jean-Pierre Blanchard believed wings and rudders helped him steer his balloon, as shown in this fanciful illustration of his English Channel flight. In truth, he had to throw these things out to keep from crashing into the water

money, and the doctor worried as the project went over budget. He wasn't as rich as people thought.

The men grew suspicious of each other. Blanchard accused Jeffries of plotting to make the flight without him. Later, Jeffries told his friends that Blanchard was the one who tried to go solo.

Jeffries's story was this: Before they flew, everything had to be weighed to make sure the balloon could lift it all. Blanchard was a very small man, but he had suddenly put on a lot of weight. It looked as if the doctor might have to stay behind.

Jeffries suspected a trick. He found it under Blanchard's coat. The little aeronaut was wearing a belt weighted with lead!

Still, both men wanted to fly across the Channel, and they had only one balloon. On the bright, chilly afternoon of January 7, 1785, they took off from Dover together.

The balloon rose slowly over the edge of a cliff. Even without Blanchard's lead belt, they were loaded with too much gear, including the useless wings and rudder that Blanchard had insisted on bringing.

As they left the white cliffs behind, they could see the coast of France, but the balloon kept sinking. It rose when they threw out sand, then sank again. All the sand was gone before they were halfway across the Channel.

They began throwing their gear overboard. When it was gone, they were still only three-quarters of the way across. Next, they threw out their ropes. Then they started taking off their clothes, because even a small difference in weight could keep them aloft a bit longer. Soon they were shivering in little more than their cork life jackets. With four or five miles to go, they sank down near the waves. It looked like the end.

Suddenly they began to rise. Perhaps it was nothing more than a current of slightly warmer air, but it was enough. Soon they were over the coast.

But they weren't out of danger. After rising high, they began falling fast toward the ground . . . and they had nothing left to throw out to slow their fall.

Then Jeffries had an idea: he needed to go to the bathroom.

Attached to the basket were some air-filled bladders, meant to help the basket float in case of a water landing. The men grabbed a few of these, emptied their own bladders into them, and tossed them overboard. Look out below!

It worked. The balloon slowed and came gently down into some trees. Grabbing branches, they walked the balloon over the treetops until they found an open place to land. A search party found them, gave them clothes, and took them to the nearest town.

France celebrated the two men as heroes. Blanchard, of course, felt he deserved all the credit. Jeffries published an account of the flight in which he praised "my gallant little captain." Out of embarrassment, Jeffries didn't mention his own contribution to their safe landing.

SOPHIE

THE CHANNEL FLIGHT brought Jean-Pierre Blanchard fame but not fortune—not fortune that he kept, anyway. He always seemed to spend more than he earned. He traveled Europe and America, flying balloons for money wherever he could. At home in France, his first wife, Victoire, died in poverty.

Later, he met a young Frenchwoman named Marie-Madeleine-Sophie Armand. When they married, he was in his forties and she was still a teenager. Some sources say she was nineteen; others say sixteen. Such age differences between husband and wife were common in those days.

Sophie was a tiny, frail-looking woman. People said she was nervous. Small noises frightened her. She even hated carriage rides because she feared the carriage would overturn.

About the last thing you'd expect Sophie to do would be to risk her life in a balloon. But several years after marrying Jean-Pierre, that's just what she did.

She discovered something about herself: she loved venturing into the sky. It was, she said, an "incomparable sensation." People described her features as "bird-like"; now, like a bird, she felt more at home in the air than on the ground.

Sophie made her first solo flight in 1805, when she was twenty-seven. She wasn't the first woman to fly, but she was the first to pilot her own balloon.

Two years later, she and Jean-Pierre were launching a hot-air balloon when it was caught in swirling winds and torn open on tree branches. Jean-Pierre fell from the basket, landed on a rooftop, and then tumbled to the ground. He was knocked out cold.

Sophie, meanwhile, landed in a tree. The branches broke her fall, but she was so shocked by what happened to her husband that she was unable to speak. But that time, Jean-Pierre recovered from his injuries.

If Sophie had been as timid as people thought, she'd have given up ballooning. But she seemed more troubled by her husband's injuries than by her own narrow escape. She kept flying.

SOPHIE'S VOW

THEN CAME JEAN-PIERRE'S STROKE and subsequent crash landing in Holland in 1809. As we've seen, he couldn't imagine that Sophie could get by without him.

After his death, Sophie didn't believe she was helpless. Others saw that she feared many things (on the ground, anyway), but she saw herself as strong—and stubborn as a goat.

And she knew why. In her day, babies were sometimes suckled on goat's milk instead of their mother's milk. Sophie had been nursed this way. She thought this had given her a goat's famous stubbornness.

Jean-Pierre had struggled for years to make a living as a balloonist. Not only was Sophie the first woman to take up this profession, she also vowed to pay off all her husband's debts. In this way she would restore honor to the Blanchard name.

She found ways to save money. With no children or husband to care for, she lived simply—no new clothes, no luxuries like coffee. She redesigned her ballooning equipment to make everything smaller and lighter. To ride in, she had a tiny, boat-shaped wicker basket made. It wasn't much bigger than a chair, but she flew alone and it was all she needed.

For gas, she preferred hydrogen to hot air. Hydrogen's greater lift was part of the reason: it allowed her to ride balloons that were little more than twenty feet in diameter.

At this point, it's worth saying just a little about hydrogen and how it's made. The balloonists in the rest of this book used hydrogen, and now and then the gas's characteristics will make a difference in the story.

First, you don't really *make* hydrogen. It's a natural element, the lightest gas there is. Finding it is easy: it's in every drop of water. Water's chemical name is H_2O, because each molecule is made of two parts hydrogen and one part oxygen.

The trick is to separate them. The key, strangely enough, is rusty iron.

Rust is what happens when oxygen molecules attach themselves to metal. By Sophie's day, scientists had learned to speed up the process by passing steam over iron filings. The steam's oxygen bonds with the iron, leaving the hydrogen to float free. Professor Charles did something similar with iron and acid.

But however you "made" hydrogen, the equipment and iron and workers cost a lot of money. Sophie got paid for her balloon flights, but she in turn had to pay for hydrogen. She made sure her balloons didn't need much.

For our purposes, there's just one other important thing about hydrogen: it burns. That's why Rozier's combination hydrogen-and-hot-air balloon was so dangerous. Having fire anywhere near a hydrogen balloon can be deadly.

INDESTRUCTIBLE

BEFORE A FLIGHT IN GERMANY IN 1810, Sophie didn't have enough hydrogen even for her small balloon. She decided to go up anyway. She hated to disappoint a crowd.

But there was only one way to lighten the balloon. Under the bag itself hung a wooden ring to which her little basket was tied. She removed the basket and sat on the ring. To the crowd's astonishment, she rose into the sky with her feet dangling over empty space.

A strong wind came up and blew her over some mountains. She spent two hours in the air, and it was dark before the balloon came down in a forest.

Sophie spent a cold night tangled in tree branches. When peasants found her the next morning, the balloon was covered with ice—and Sophie was nearly frozen herself.

Madame Blanchard in her balloon basket in Italy, 1811

The following year, Sophie canceled a flight in Rome because of bad weather. The weather was just as bad the next day, but she refused to cancel two days in a row. She launched from an amphitheater in a high wind. As the balloon slammed wildly around the arena, spectators tried to catch the ropes to rescue her.

But Sophie, stubbornly, didn't want to be rescued. Up she went, colliding with rooftops until finally rising clear of the city.

Jean-Pierre had always said that the only thing his wife truly feared was drowning . . . and now Sophie came down in the Tiber River. Swept along by the current, she grabbed hold of a branch and pulled herself ashore. She was battered and bleeding, but not seriously hurt.

However, these wild flights were exceptions. Most of the time things went smoothly, and Sophie gained a reputation for reliability. The public came to love and respect her more than they had her boastful husband. She was honorable, successful, and generous. As she promised, she paid off all of Jean-Pierre's debts—even though she didn't have to. She made a comfortable living for herself, and donated some of her money to disaster victims.

Everyone was shocked and saddened, then, when word of her disappearance reached Paris in 1811. Her balloon had come down with some food and extra clothing in the basket, but no Sophie. She must have fallen to her death.

But no sooner did the news reach Paris than Sophie herself arrived, unharmed. She said she'd landed in the country because there was no wind to carry her farther. She had begun walking toward the nearest town, but the wind blew again and carried the balloon miles away . . . and that's when people saw it land without her.

Everyone was relieved. The famous Madame Blanchard seemed indestructible.

THE FIERY STAR

THESE WERE THE YEARS when Napoleon Bonaparte ruled France. He was one of the most famous men in history, a conquering general who made himself emperor.

Napoleon enjoyed lavish celebrations in his honor. In 1811, he hosted an event that drew 300,000 people. He spared no expense. People walked among fountains, tables of food, and trees hung with colored glass. Actors, musicians, jugglers, and acrobats performed for the crowd. Gunboats carried out naval maneuvers on the river. And the grand finale was a balloon ascension by Madame Blanchard.

That night, Sophie introduced something new to her performance. Her crew let the balloon up on ropes so everyone could see her. When they cut the ropes, Sophie lit a fuse. As she rose into the air, the fuse burned down to a large fireworks star hanging thirty feet below her basket.

The crowd watched in awe as Sophie passed over their heads, clearly visible by the light of the fireworks. She was wearing a white dress and a white cap with ostrich feathers, and waving a flag. Her star trailed a shower of sparks like a comet.

"She appeared as if sailing in a chariot of fire at immense height," said one witness. "I imagined myself in fairyland."

During the years 1812–19, Sophie was the most famous and popular balloonist in the world. She was in charge of royal balloon ascensions, and every couple of weeks she performed at Tivoli Gardens, a public garden in Paris.

The fiery star became her trademark. Sparks of gold, silver, red, blue, and green showered down for about five minutes as her balloon rose higher and higher into the black sky. Then the star went dim and Sophie vanished into the night.

Audiences loved it, but anyone could see that it was dangerous. For one thing, landing at night means landing blind. It's hard to know if you're coming down into water or trees or some other bad place—until it's too late.

But Sophie preferred night flights. People even said she liked to curl up and sleep in her little basket as she sailed through the darkness toward morning.

The other danger, of course, was the fireworks. One mistake and her balloon would burst into flame like a giant torch. Sophie understood this. She was careful, and she felt the show was worth it.

THE GRAND FINALE

On July 6, 1819, Sophie prepared for another flight at Tivoli. Because a big celebration was going on, she planned a surprise for her grand finale. It was a parachute loaded with fireworks. She would release it after her flaming star burned out. It would go off right when everyone thought the show was over.

Afterward, people said that Sophie was more nervous than usual that evening. Some knew of the extra fireworks and warned against it. Others told her to go ahead. She hesitated. Then she sprang into her basket.

"Let's go," she said. "This will be for the last time."

And maybe it really happened that way. Or maybe that's just how people chose to remember the launch of Sophie Blanchard's sixty-seventh balloon flight—as if they had known what was about to happen.

The performance began the usual way: Sophie, dressed in white, rose higher and higher while the orchestra played, the crowd cheered, and fireworks lit up the sky. Then she vanished into a cloud.

When she reappeared, there came a flash of light, then a jet of fire shooting from the balloon. The crowd applauded.

"*Brava!*" they shouted. "*Vive Madame Blanchard!*"

But as the flames spread, the shouts of joy turned to cries of horror. Sophie was struggling to close the neck of the balloon where the hydrogen was burning.

But the fire was out of control. Sophie could do no more, and she sat down while the fire raged above her. As the hydrogen burned, the balloon began to sink, slowly at first, then faster and faster.

It landed on a rooftop. Some eyewitnesses said the rush of air against the falling balloon had put out the fire. Whether it did or not, one thing is clear: Sophie was still alive.

But as the balloon dragged across the roof, the basket suddenly overturned on an iron bar, pitching Sophie out. Onlookers heard her cry "Help!" as she slid off the roof and fell headfirst to the street below.

And it was this final misfortune that killed her. If the basket hadn't overturned, France would probably have celebrated yet another daring escape by its aerial heroine.

As it was, the nation mourned. That night, the Tivoli audience took up a collection for Sophie's children. Soon, they learned that the forty-one-year-old aeronaut didn't have any. In her will, Sophie left her substantial fortune to a friend's seven-year-old daughter.

We don't know for sure how the fire started. Some said Sophie's fireworks brushed against trees on the way up, causing some of her rockets to shoot toward her balloon instead of away from it. Others thought leaking hydrogen caught fire when she lit the second batch of fireworks.

For years afterward, writers had little to say about Sophie Blanchard's amazing career. When they wrote of her at all, it was usually only to describe her tragic death. To some, the story taught a lesson about the folly of a woman doing a man's work. They chose not to notice that all balloonists took risks, and that Sophie Blanchard faced hers with arguably greater skill and courage than any man of her time.

Of countless photos of American aircraft, this is probably the first. John Steiner prepares his balloon in Erie, Pennsylvania, hoping to become the first person to fly across Lake Erie

SPLASHDOWN IN LAKE ERIE

JOHN STEINER (UNITED STATES, 1857)

JOHN STEINER LOOKED UP AT THE SKY, frowning. What had promised to be a fine spring day had suddenly turned stormy. Rain drenched the crowd that had turned out to watch him launch his balloon. A circle of men struggled to hold the balloon down against gale-force winds.

And out on Lake Erie, the wind was whipping the gray water into white-caps. Steiner planned to fly his balloon forty miles over that lake, from Erie, Pennsylvania, to the Canadian shore. No one had ever tried it, and right now it didn't look like such a good idea.

But Steiner stayed with his balloon, hoping for a break in the weather. The crowd stayed, too, with hats and bonnets dripping, and hoopskirts sagging under the weight of rainwater. A photograph taken that day shows the balloon being inflated on a city street. Oblong in shape and already as tall as a two-story building, it looked like a giant grape.

Steiner had come to America from Germany just four years earlier. He lived in Philadelphia and toured the country flying balloons. This was his fortieth flight—and the most dangerous journey he had yet attempted.

At about half past three, the clouds broke and the wind died down. Steiner climbed into his basket and gave the order to cut loose.

As he rose slowly above the buildings, Steiner waved a flag with one hand and his cap with the other. The crowd cheered him again and again. Rising too slowly, he threw out a bag of ballast and shot upward. After four minutes in the air, he vanished into the clouds.

The people of Erie stood staring upward. The threat of violent weather was by no means over. But five minutes later, they spotted the balloon through a break in the heavy clouds. Steiner was heading northeast across the lake, just as he'd intended.

"If he met no counter currents, he undoubtedly landed safe in her Majesty's dominions before dark," said the *Erie Observer* two days later.

Because even then, Erie had no news of Steiner's whereabouts. The *Observer* guessed that he probably came down in a part of Canada "where telegraphs have not penetrated." But no one in Erie knew for sure.

The newspaper seemed unaware of two things: first, that Steiner's late departure meant that if anything went wrong, he might not reach land before nightfall; and second, that a powerful storm had struck the northern part of Lake Erie that evening.

AMONG THE STORM CLOUDS

SAILING HIGH OVER THE LAKE, Steiner watched Erie recede behind him. The city seemed to be "going down, down" and the people looked like "little black pins on a cushion," he said later. He felt a "dreary sense of loneliness."

His spirits rose with his balloon. Soon he was three miles high and sailing swiftly toward Canada. Through gaps in the clouds, he could see clear across the lake, and for much of its east-west length, too. He counted thirty-eight ships on the water. Now and then he heard the faraway voices of sailors cheering him on.

And then the storm clouds closed in. To Steiner, they looked like "mountains enveloped in mist" or "gigantic phantoms."

Flying over a thunderstorm isn't the same as standing under one. John Wise (an aeronaut we'll meet in a later chapter, "The Long Voyage") said that a storm cloud doesn't look dark from above. Instead, it is so dazzlingly white in the sunshine that it hurts to look at one.

"And then it heaves and rolls about like the boisterous ocean," he wrote, or like "a great bubbling, boiling cauldron of snow." The cloud builds and builds, then "suddenly melts down again" as it dumps a torrent of rain. Sailing above, you might not see the rain, but you hear it rushing like a giant waterfall somewhere below.

Then there's the lightning. When you're floating among the clouds, the air is so quiet (at least when it's not raining) that you can hear the steady beat of your own pulse. Suddenly, a cloud flashes nearby. A clap of thunder shakes you in your boots—but it isn't the deep, booming thunder you might expect. Up here, Wise said, thunder is "a snarling crash," like a rifle shot.

With all that electricity in the air, your compass needle no longer points north. Instead, it dances wildly around the dial, pointing to one churning cloud after another.

"Then you are in a wilderness," Wise said. "As far as knowing your whereabouts is concerned, you may be considered lost in the desert. Your compass does no more good than a jack-o'-lantern to direct you."

Steiner could only watch and hope.

"Oh! What a scene was transpiring around me!" he said later. "Every moment the surrounding masses of clouds were illuminated by flashes of lightning, succeeded by terrible crashes of thunder, in the very midst of which I seemed to be floating." He imagined he could "feel my frail car quiver at every shock."

At last he caught a glimpse of the Canadian shore. It was only about three miles away!

But to his horror, the shore grew farther and farther away. The wind had changed. He was being blown back out over the lake!

Forty years after Steiner's Lake Erie flight, French aeronaut Félix Nadar pilots a balloon from a basket equipped like the ones used in Steiner's day

THE SHIP AND THE COMET

ABOARD THE STEAMSHIP MARY STEWART, Captain Woodruff didn't know what to make of a small speck in the sky. It was high and far away, up near a black cloud. At first he thought it might be a gull.

The deckhands had another idea, and it frightened them. Earlier that year, word had spread that a comet was going to strike the earth on June 13. It was going to be the end of the world.

Though scientists tried to debunk the rumor, many people in Europe and North America worried that the end was near. Years later, a French astronomer remembered how people in Paris started watching the planet Venus in February. They mistook it for a comet and imagined that they could see a comet's tail.

By the time of Steiner's flight on June 18, the earth-destroying comet was five days overdue. But when the crewmen saw a strange object in the sky, they didn't know what else it might be. It didn't occur to them that someone might be crazy enough to fly a balloon in such weather. In their minds, the dreaded comet was coming at last, hurtling through the sky like a steam locomotive at full throttle.

The captain called for his telescope. He saw at once that the mysterious object was a manned balloon. Captain Woodruff knew something about storms on Lake Erie . . . and he knew that the man in the basket was in deep trouble.

Steiner spotted the *Mary Stewart* at around the same time. The ship was about two and a half miles below him, and fifteen miles distant.

The wind was carrying the balloon toward Buffalo, New York, at the east end of the lake. Despite his speed, Steiner knew he wouldn't get there before dark. Landing there would mean crashing blindly into who-knows-what at sixty or seventy miles per hour.

And he might not make the shore at all. The wind had already played one cruel trick on him. It might play another.

In desperation, Steiner leaps from the balloon. From Frank Leslie's Illustrated Newspaper, *July 4, 1857*

Then Steiner heard the ship's whistle and saw the crew hoisting a flag. They had seen him! He knew that the tiny-looking ship on the storm-tossed waves was now his best chance for survival. He waved a flag in reply, and then pulled the valve rope. He began coming down fast.

IN THE WAVES

STEINER HIT THE WATER about a mile short of the ship—or three miles, depending on which newspaper you read.

On impact, he was buried beneath the waves. Then the wind filled the sagging balloon like a sail, tearing it from the water and dragging Steiner and the basket with it. Luckily for the aeronaut, the wind carried his craft in the right direction. The balloon bounced toward the ship, splashing down and tearing away repeatedly. Each time, it rose twenty to perhaps a hundred feet in the air before hitting the water again.

Gasping for breath when he came to the surface, Steiner held on. He simply had to reach the ship. Even if by some miracle the balloon were to settle in the water and stay put, he might not survive for long.

"The open wicker car is the worst possible boat for the luckless voyagers," wrote British aeronaut John Bacon years later. Yet "to leave it and cling to the rigging is but a forlorn hope" because the netting around the balloon "would prove a death-trap in the water. There are many instances of lives having been lost in such a dilemma, even when help was near at hand."

After seven agonizing minutes, Steiner passed near the ship. A rowboat was waiting for him. The deckhands—the same men who'd just been terrified by the "comet"—were now about to risk their lives for a man they'd never met.

An anchor line trailed from the balloon. The crewmen grabbed hold of it and tied it to their boat. The balloon towed them through the water at high speed.

Steiner leaped from the basket. He swam toward the oncoming boat. Soon, strong hands lifted him over the side.

The balloon was still towing the boat away from the ship. Seeing this, Captain Woodruff shouted for the men to untie the rope from the boat's bow (or front) and tie it to the stern (back). He wanted them to row against the balloon's pull until the ship could reach them.

The men tried this, but the balloon tore the rope from their hands. Free of its extra weight, the balloon shot into the sky and vanished in the storm.

The men rowed back to the ship, where Steiner impressed the captain with the way he "sat down to supper as if nothing had happened." Though he'd barely escaped death, the only thing that seemed to bother him was the loss of his five-hundred-dollar balloon.

He got it back. Later the tattered craft was found in Canada. It had completed the journey without him!

A balloon water rescue could hold its own against the most sensational news of the day. An 1874 balloon rescue appeared in a British illustrated newspaper . . . alongside a gruesome tale of murder

THE COUNT

STEINER WENT ON to other adventures. In 1858, he defeated a famous European balloonist in the "Great Balloon Race" in Cincinnati. Each man flew as far as he could. Steiner won by flying 230 miles.

He tried another Great Lakes crossing the year after that. This time he flew nearly the entire length of Lake Ontario, 160 miles, from Toronto, Ontario, to Oswego, New York.

During the Civil War, Steiner and several other aeronauts offered their services to the Union Army. They went up in tethered balloons to watch and report on enemy armies. Sometimes it worked well, but even then the army often ignored the balloon men. The army didn't always pay them, either. Frustrated, Steiner resigned and went home.

The war raged on, but Steiner was far away from it by the summer of 1863. He flew for paying audiences in Minnesota. He even took up passengers on tethered flights.

One day in St. Paul, a young German army officer paid for a ride. He had come to America as a military observer and was touring the country. He was also a count, part of his country's nobility. No doubt he was pleased to find another man who could speak German.

As they rose into the air, the count saw immediately how useful a balloon could be to an army. Not only could you see what your enemy was doing, but you could also tell your artillery just where to shoot.

Steiner agreed, but he told the count of a time when his balloon got loose and floated right over the Confederate army. He had a good view of the enemy, but was lucky not to be captured.

The problem, Steiner said, is that it's hard to control a balloon when it's not tied down. He described a long, narrow balloon that he wanted to build, one with a rudder to steer it. The young count listened with interest.

Steiner never built his special balloon. Eventually he retired and disappeared from history. He wasn't the first person to propose a dirigible (a steerable balloon), but his conversation in the sky above St. Paul was more important than he knew. Many years later, his passenger—Count Ferdinand von Zeppelin—became famous for building giant airships. (That is how "zeppelin" became another word for airship.)

But the count said he first got the idea on the day he took a balloon ride with John Steiner.

Local people come running after a balloon lands—as people did when an aeronaut landed his balloon at the Harvey farm in Illinois in 1858

THE CHILDREN ARE GONE!

MARTHA AND DAVID HARVEY (UNITED STATES, 1858)

BY NOW YOU KNOW why balloon flights were so popular. Part of it was the sense of danger. There was something unnatural about going up in the sky.

And if you wanted to tell a scary story, a good choice was to talk about someone who went up in a balloon by accident, with no one aboard to help.

Such accidents were rare, but they were the stuff of legend.

In Illinois in 1858, this very thing happened to an eight-year-old girl named Martha Harvey and her three-year-old brother, David. They found themselves up in a balloon in the dark of night . . . and all alone.

LET'S TAKE A RIDE

IT ALL STARTED ON SEPTEMBER 17, when aeronaut Silas Brooks found himself too ill to keep a scheduled appearance. A man named Samuel Wilson volunteered to go in his place. Wilson took off from the southern Illinois town of Centralia. That evening he came down twenty miles to the southeast.

As for what happened next, maybe it would have been the same if Brooks had been there. Or Brooks might have been more careful about who handled the balloon once it landed.

Wilson came down in a tree on Benjamin Harvey's farm. The family and neighbors came to help. Soon, the balloon was out of the tree and Wilson was on the ground chatting with people, enjoying the attention.

Meanwhile, Mr. Harvey and some others towed the balloon over to the farmhouse. Harvey had decided he was going to have some fun. He told the others to hold the rope while he climbed into the basket. He wanted them to let the balloon up the length of the rope, then haul him back down.

Martha Harvey, age eight, and her brother, David, three, sat for a portrait after their rescue. From Frank Leslie's Illustrated Newspaper, *October 23, 1858*

Harvey wasn't a big man, but he was too heavy for the balloon to rise. No matter—he'd let his three kids take a ride instead. He put them in the basket.

Wilson saw what was happening. He didn't mind, but shouted for the men to be sure to hang on to that rope.

But the balloon still wouldn't rise. Together the three children were too heavy. So the older daughter climbed out, leaving Martha and David.

Significantly lighter, the balloon suddenly shot upward. Despite Wilson's warning, the men did not have a grip on the rope! At the end of the line, the balloon's anchor caught in a wooden rail fence, but tore right through it.

"Pull me down, Father!" the children cried—but already their voices were growing fainter as they flew swiftly into the sky.

It was past seven o'clock and getting dark. The balloon rose almost straight up, and then began floating away to the southeast.

Then it was gone, and Martha and David with it.

MISSING

MR. AND MRS. HARVEY WERE FRANTIC. No one knew which way the wind would blow as the balloon rose higher, so they sent out messengers in all directions. For miles around, groups of men and boys walked the countryside and searched the woods.

The balloon would come down, but where? The children might land in a river and drown. Or they could crash in deep woods and starve to death before anyone found them.

Newspaper readers already knew the story of Michigan balloonist Ira Thurston, missing since August 16.

Like Martha and David's, Thurston's last flight was an accident. After landing safely, he tried a common but dangerous maneuver to empty his balloon of hydrogen. He removed the basket, climbed on top of the balloon, and then told people holding the ropes to let go. When they did, his weight flipped the balloon upside down.

That's just what he wanted. With the balloon's open neck pointing skyward, the gas would rush out quickly.

But the neck was tangled in ropes. The gas stayed inside, and the balloon floated away. Thurston was last seen clinging desperately to the netting.

The aeronaut Thurston clings to his balloon. He was still missing when the Harvey children disappeared. He went accidentally aloft without a basket

The balloon was found in Canada several days later—without Thurston.

Back in Centralia, word spread quickly of a new aerial tragedy, this time involving local children. People called Silas Brooks from his sickbed to tell him the news.

Brooks tried to comfort the public. He said the balloon would probably come down in two or three hours, and within thirty miles of where it started. (This would create a search area of 2,800 square miles, but he probably didn't tell them that part.)

He also sent word to the parents. He said the children were in little danger . . . unless they came down in the woods, where they'd be hard to find. Or one child might step out of the basket first, in which case the lightened balloon would carry the other child back into the sky.

We don't know how comforting this was to Mr. and Mrs. Harvey. But other people said that the children wouldn't survive the freezing temperatures of the upper atmosphere.

Brooks hadn't said anything about that. Had he known then what he learned later, he'd have had more reason to worry.

TO DANGEROUS HEIGHTS

LET'S SKIP AHEAD, then, to a few days later, when Brooks visited the Harvey family. Only then did he realize how quickly—and how far—the balloon had gone up.

First he had to do the math. After eighty-six balloon flights, Brooks knew what he was doing. He started by estimating the balloon's lifting power—the most weight it could carry and still float above the ground.

That was easy enough. Mr. Harvey weighed 150 pounds. When he was in the basket, the balloon would only float when someone kept a hand underneath. Brooks guessed the balloon could raise at least 140 pounds by itself.

To fly, a balloon's lifting power needs to be greater than the weight it carries—but not much greater. For safety's sake, Brooks always added sandbags until the balloon, basket, and passengers together weighed only four to six pounds less than the balloon's lifting power. That way it would rise gently, instead of shooting quickly to dangerous heights.

But Martha and David together weighed only about eighty pounds. Instead of a safe four- to six-pound difference between lift and weight, the difference was sixty pounds. That's why the balloon had shot upward so quickly.

Based on his experience, Brooks knew that a balloon with that much lift would soar at least four and a half miles high—more than 23,000 feet—before coming down. By comparison, the highest mountain in North America (Alaska's Mount McKinley) stands 20,320 feet tall.

It was a good thing that nobody knew that yet during the long night of September 17–18. They knew Martha and David were somewhere up in the night sky, all alone. That was worry enough for the time being.

THE FIERY DRAGON

As HER HOME AND FAMILY sank quickly below her, Martha called to her father to pull them back down. Soon she saw it was no use. Her house looked like a doll's house, and the little crowd of people beside it shrank to insect size.

According to one report, they passed over a town and Martha called for help, but by then they were so high that no one heard her.

As the sky around them grew dark and chilly, Martha could do little but try to comfort her brother. He was crying and shivering with the cold. Martha took off her apron and wrapped it around him.

Framing the dark bulk of the balloon above them, the sky was inky black and full of stars . . . and a comet. No one was predicting the end of the world this time, but Donati's Comet was real.

One newspaper wrote of the children's reaction—though the conversation might be made up. Newspapers did that sometimes to make a story more colorful. In this case, the newspaper in question didn't even get the children's names right.

Even so, it might be true that David saw the comet and worried aloud that this fiery dragon might come too near, setting their balloon on fire with a mighty swish of its tail.

And it might be true that Martha assured him that the dragon was "as much as twenty miles away" and that anyway God wouldn't let it hurt them.

The story goes on to say that Martha's words calmed David. But then he said, "I wish it would come a little nearer, so I could warm myself—I'm so cold!"

What's more certain is that David fell asleep, and that Martha was left to watch the blazing comet. She saw, too, the many meteors that traced bright paths in the sky that night (people still call them "shooting stars"). She probably knew little about comets or meteors, and may have wondered if they might indeed strike the balloon and set it on fire.

Martha didn't know very much about balloons, either, and Mr. Brooks wasn't there to tell her that she would likely come down soon. Shivering and breathing deeply in the thin air, she knew that no grownup could help her.

Then she saw a rope dangling from the balloon's open neck. She didn't know what it was for, but she guessed correctly that it had something to do with controlling the balloon.

She pulled the rope and released it. Somewhere above her, the valve door opened and slapped shut again.

But a more meaningful sound came from the countryside far below. Martha realized she could hear roosters crowing more plainly after she pulled the rope. With no lights on the ground to guide her, it was too dark to see—but she knew the balloon was coming down at last.

After that, she hung on the valve rope until she heard the snapping of branches and felt the basket scraping and jostling. She was near the ground, but not near enough. Now they were stuck high in a tree, with no way to get down!

THE COMET SPEAKS

IGNATIUS ATCHISON crawled out of bed at three in the morning. He wanted to see the comet. Astronomers had said that viewing would be best at that hour.

Atchison lived seventeen miles southeast of the Harvey place, but he didn't know about the balloon or the missing children. He stepped out onto his front porch, felt the chilly night air . . . and stopped in his tracks.

One newspaper described what he saw

After the tethered balloon they were in got away, the Harvey children flew well into the night—then were stuck in a tree until they were discovered. From Frank Leslie's Illustrated Newspaper, *October 23, 1858*

as "an immense specter"—a ghost—"rising from a tree about twenty yards distant."

Other reports say that Atchison thought it was the comet come to earth, and that he panicked when he heard it crying out to him with a human voice.

Whatever he thought, he ran back inside and woke up the rest of the family. Something strange had landed in the yard.

Going back outside, Atchison heard the voice again. It was a child's voice. It spoke to him clearly: "Come here and let us down! We are almost frozen!"

Then he understood. And as Donati's Comet blazed in the night sky 52 million miles away, the Atchison family began cutting away tree branches so they could reach the children.

Morning came before they hauled the basket down from the tree. Three-year-old David was the first one out. Safe on the ground, he ran several steps. Then he turned suddenly and looked back at the balloon with wonder.

They lifted Martha out, and she told them her story. She and her brother had spent more than thirteen hours in the balloon basket.

It took a day for the news to reach Centralia, where the balloon had started out before it came to the Harvey farm. Churches announced it on Sunday morning "amid ecstasies of joy," as the papers reported it.

And when Martha and David arrived in Centralia on Monday, the town welcomed them with "the firing of cannon and a general jubilee." A photographer took the children's portrait, and townspeople gave them presents.

The Harvey children had been fortunate. They could easily have come to a tragic end, as did Ira Thurston. The following March, his bones were finally discovered in a Michigan forest. He had clung to his balloon for ten miles before he fell. By the time he was found, only his clothing and the contents of his pockets identified him.

But for Martha and David, accidental flight was the adventure of a lifetime. They were ordinary children before; suddenly everyone regarded them with wonder. Even if they never flew again, they were aeronauts now—and the youngest ever.

After crashing through the woods near the shore of Lake Ontario, the balloon Atlantic *came to rest in the treetops after a stormy flight from St. Louis*

THE LONG VOYAGE

THE FLIGHT OF THE BALLOON *ATLANTIC* (UNITED STATES, 1859)

YOUNG JOHN WISE LOVED THE SKY. At night, he used to lie outside on a straw heap for hours, looking up at the moon and stars.

By day, his favorite toy was a kite. He even built one that carried his pet kitten as a passenger. Sometimes he flew her so high that she disappeared in the clouds. How he wished she "could speak and tell me how it looked from on high!"

Maybe she'd have told him to risk his own life next time and leave her out of it—which was just what he wanted to do. He wanted to build a kite big enough to carry himself. But it would be too expensive.

Wise was born in Lancaster, Pennsylvania, in 1808. He began flying kites back when Sophie Blanchard was thrilling European audiences with her aerial fireworks.

Wise didn't know of her at the time. He first learned of ballooning when he was fourteen and read about European aeronauts in his father's German newspapers.

Soon he built his own balloon. It was a miniature montgolfier that carried its own fire in a little basket. It soared several hundred feet in the air, then landed on a thatched roof and set it on fire. Bells rang all over town, and the fire brigade passed buckets to douse the flames. Trembling, Wise watched from behind a window as the firemen saved the building. He was in big trouble.

John Wise was the best-known American aeronaut of his generation

That misadventure put an end to Wise's ballooning for many years. He grew up and became a piano maker, but he never forgot his youthful dreams. When he was twenty-seven, he built and piloted a full-size balloon. Soon he was performing for paying audiences.

By 1859, "Professor" John Wise was fifty-one years old. With more than two hundred flights to his credit, he was America's most experienced aeronaut. But he dreamed of something bigger, a journey more daring than anything yet attempted.

THE TRANS-ATLANTIC BALLOON COMPANY

JOHN LA MOUNTAIN was a sailor lured from the sea to the sky. John Wise sold him his first balloon. In 1859, La Mountain was twenty-nine years old and a veteran of a half-dozen flights.

He and Wise shared a dream. They both believed that a balloon could cross the Atlantic Ocean from America to Europe. Between three and four miles above the earth, Wise found a constant east-to-west wind that blew fifty to eighty miles an hour. Riding that current, Europe was only a few days away—instead of weeks by ship.

Wise had once asked Congress for $20,000 to build a balloon large enough to make the journey. They'd all but laughed at him. Now young and inexperienced La Mountain succeeded where Wise had failed. A man named O. A. Gager agreed to finance his $30,000 balloon.

With advice from Wise, La Mountain built a balloon that stood sixty feet tall and could lift 25,000 pounds—including a sixteen-foot lifeboat hanging below its wicker basket. The balloon's name (and purpose) appeared in bold letters on the silk fabric: *ATLANTIC*.

Gager and La Mountain then invited Wise and other investors to form the Trans-Atlantic Balloon Company. They dreamed of carrying mail and passengers to the cities of Europe.

First, however, they planned a flight from St. Louis to New York. No one in America had flown so far before, but half a continent looks small compared to an ocean. It was to be merely a test flight, a warm-up to the main event.

Balloonist John La Mountain was one of Wise's partners in the Atlantic *flight. The two men were jealous of each other, and bickered long after the flight*

THE SAFEST MODE OF TRAVEL KNOWN

UNDER A BLAZING SUN ON JULY 1, 1859, workers loaded the *Atlantic* with food, drink, and a thousand pounds of sand ballast. Wise climbed up to the basket; La Mountain, Gager, and a newspaper reporter named William Hyde stayed below in the boat. Wise would pull the valve rope when they sailed too high; La Mountain would drop ballast when they sank too low.

Thousands of people cheered from streets, open lots, and rooftops as the *Atlantic* sailed away into the evening sky. The four men looked down upon the broad Mississippi River and watched St. Louis fade under the mantle of smoke that covered all cities in those days. The western sky turned gold and purple, and a thin crescent moon settled slowly to the horizon.

"I do not think I ever before experienced such exhilaration of spirit—such real joy," wrote Hyde, who was taking his first balloon ride. "My feeling was that ballooning, beside being the most pleasant and swift, was the safest mode of travel known."

And the stars came out, bright and multicolored. When the balloon passed over a lake, the men saw stars both above and below, as if they were sailing through outer space.

Wise became sleepy. Telling the others to wake him when he was needed, he curled up in the basket. The balloon rose high and the air grew cold. Soon the men called for Wise to open the valve and bring them down a bit. He didn't respond.

They called again. No reply.

They called a third time. Still no reply.

Finally, Gager climbed up to the basket—and was shocked to find Wise unconscious and breathing in spasms.

It had been a simple mistake. Like all hydrogen balloons, the *Atlantic* had an open neck so gas could escape if it got too full. In this case the neck ended in a long hose that hung over the side of the basket. As the balloon climbed higher and the gas expanded, the swelling balloon pulled the hose right over Wise's face. He was being smothered by hydrogen.

Gager removed the hose. Slowly, the professor came to.

"A few minutes more would have ended my existence," he said later. It "felt like a sleep of years."

He had been dreaming of interplanetary balloon voyages.

The first crisis had passed. The men didn't know it yet, but they were flying toward far greater danger.

ACROSS LAKE ERIE

UNLESS YOU'VE BEEN FAR from the bright lights that illuminate our homes and neighborhoods at night—out on the ocean or in some remote part of the world—it's hard to appreciate how dark it used to get after the sun set.

For the men of the *Atlantic*, the colorful stars and black sky came partly from the altitude (less atmosphere blocking the view between them and outer space), but mostly it was because electric lights hadn't been invented. Even cities lit by gaslight were far away. Beneath the balloon, the land was a dark void.

The best way to learn what was below was to ask the dogs. Now and then, one of the men would call a loud "Halloooo!" into the darkness. When hundreds of dogs barked in reply, it meant the balloon was over a town. A handful of dogs indicated a farm, and a lone dog probably guarded an isolated log cabin in the woods. What a lonely trip it would be over the ocean, where there were no dogs at all!

As the gray light of early morning crept upon them, the men didn't know quite where they were—Indiana, they believed. Maybe Ohio. A little before sunrise, they passed a city they guessed was Fort Wayne.

Wise said nothing, but he was starting to worry about the weather. Though the sky was clear, the wind and barometer made him think the day might turn stormy. La Mountain, the sailor, may have thought the same thing, but likewise held his tongue.

A little after sunrise, the northeast sky began glaring "like white-hot metal," in Wise's words. Squinting, the men puzzled over it. Hyde and Gager found an umbrella to shade themselves. Then someone suggested that it must be reflected sunlight from some massive body of water just over the horizon.

Lake Erie! They couldn't see it, but they were heading straight for it.

They were over the water by seven o'clock. Heavy clouds were forming to the east and south, and the rolling waves below were white with spray. Two years earlier, John Steiner had tried to cross the lake the short way, forty miles south to north across a narrow portion. Now the *Atlantic* would try to cross it the long way, 240 miles west to east.

Flying low above the waves, they overtook a steamer going in the same direction. According to Wise, someone shouted down: "How do you do, captain? A fine morning for boating."

"Good morning, my brave fellows," the astonished captain replied. "But where in heavens did you come from?"

"From St. Louis, sir, last evening."

"And pray, where are you going?"

"Going eastward, captain; first to Buffalo, and then to Europe if we can."

"Good luck to you. You are going like thunder."

But did they really have time for this whole conversation? Because the captain was right about their speed—in the furious wind, the *Atlantic* was making sixty miles an hour. The steamer was beyond shouting distance in a matter of seconds. Within half an hour it was just a speck on the horizon.

SAILING BETWEEN LIFE AND DEATH

MIGHTY NIAGARA FALLS looked puny from ten thousand feet. The *Atlantic* and her crew were riding high in triumph. They had conquered Lake Erie.

Now they faced a decision. Lake Ontario, easternmost of the Great Lakes, lay dead ahead. Ballast was running low, and the far shore was a hundred miles distant.

"Crossing the second lake would have been sheer recklessness," Hyde wrote.

The others agreed . . . to a point. They decided to touch down between the lakes, drop off Hyde and Gager, and take on more ballast. Then Wise and La Mountain would sail on for Boston or Portland on the Atlantic coast.

The plan had only one flaw. As they sank toward the ground, the men began to hear the howl of wind through the trees, and the gunshot crack of breaking limbs.

Up in the balloon, the air seemed still and quiet, but that was an illusion. The storm had come at last, and the *Atlantic* was riding it like a magic carpet. Below, the wind flattened grain in the fields. It blew apart stout rail fences as if they were made of toothpicks.

Soon the men were drawing near the swaying treetops at ninety miles an hour, Wise estimated, "sailing between life and death." He shouted down to La Mountain in the boat, "For God's sake heave overboard anything you can lay your hands on!"

La Mountain did, and the balloon cleared the trees.

"Like a bullet we shot out into the lake," Hyde wrote.

"O! how terribly it was foaming, moaning and howling," Wise wrote.

STRIKING THE WAVES

THE GRAY MILES FLEW BY and the last of the ballast went over the side. The men's gear went next, then their bottles of wine, and finally a mail-bag full of letters to New York.

As the balloon sank toward the angry waves, La Mountain sent Hyde up to join Wise and Gager in the basket. But the sailor remained in the boat.

La Mountain knew he couldn't safely launch the boat at that speed. He also knew better than to climb into the basket and cut the boat free. The loss of so much weight at once would send the balloon soaring to a tremendous height. Then it would come down quickly—probably in the lake—and they'd be worse off than before.

THE TREES

Aᴛ ʟᴀsᴛ ᴛʜᴇʏ ᴄᴀᴍᴇ ᴛᴏ Lᴀᴋᴇ Oɴᴛᴀʀɪᴏ's ᴇᴀsᴛᴇʀɴ sʜᴏʀᴇ. The sight was not reassuring. They were on a collision course with a dark forest that stood before them like a wall.

Their best chance was to ditch the balloon before reaching shore. With all four men in the basket, Hyde and La Mountain held the valve rope; Gager threw the anchor.

They weren't quick enough. They struck the ground a hundred yards inland, then crashed into the trees. The anchor caught, but its hooks snapped off one by one as the *Atlantic* bounded over and blasted through a mile of forest.

"Trees half the size of a man's body were snapped in twain as though they were pipe-stems," Hyde wrote, "and huge limbs were scattered like leaves."

Finally the basket stuck in the fork of a tree. For a moment the men waited, listening to the wind whining through the ropes and flapping the silk.

Crack! The balloon tore itself away. A tree limb weighing more than six hundred pounds now swung from the netting. Under its weight, the balloon didn't go far. Crashing into another tree, the gasbag collapsed and split open in several places. They would fly no farther.

It was 2:35 p.m. After nineteen hours and more than eight hundred miles, the flight of the *Atlantic* had ended near Henderson, New York. The men were shaken, their clothes tattered, and they hung in a basket twenty-five feet off the ground. Behind them, their route through the woods looked like the path of a tornado. But they were alive and not badly hurt.

Soon, local people braved the storm to investigate. With some amusement, Wise told of an old woman who "said she was astonished to see such a sensible-looking group riding in such an outlandish vehicle." She

64

asked where they were from. They said St. Louis. She asked how far that was. They said it was about a thousand miles.

That's when she knew they were telling tales. Wise said she "looked very suspiciously over the top of her spectacles, and said, 'That will do now.'"

THE GREATEST VOYAGE

WISE CALLED IT "the greatest balloon voyage that was ever made." He had a point. The *Atlantic* set an American distance record that stood for sixty-one years, until 1910.

But within weeks, Wise and La Mountain were sniping at each other in newspaper articles. They argued over who deserved credit or blame for the flight. Both said they were going to attempt trans-Atlantic voyages. Neither ever did.

Later that year, La Mountain took the patched-up *Atlantic* for a test flight in upstate New York. He and a partner were blown deep into the Canadian wilderness. They barely survived the long march home.

Wise kept flying into his seventies, but pressed his luck with the Great Lakes once too often. He disappeared over Lake Michigan in 1879. He was never seen again.

The aeronauts' dream of trans-Atlantic flight was eventually fulfilled, but not as they expected. They didn't live to see the balloon *Double Eagle II*, which landed safely in France after a 137-hour flight from Maine. By then it was 1978, and airplanes had been crossing the ocean for years.

Coxwell and Glaisher released pigeons during their flight to more than 30,000 feet high.
One flies away; one is already dead

TO THE TOP OF THE SKY

HENRY COXWELL was nine years old when he first watched a balloon through his father's telescope. Like John Wise, he thought about balloons for years before he finally flew in one as an adult. He thought his parents wouldn't approve, so he made his first professional flights under the name "Henry Wells." But in time, Coxwell's name grew to be as well known in Britain as Wise's was in America.

In 1848, Coxwell helped an aeronaut named Gypson with an aerial fireworks display. Soon after they set off the fireworks, Coxwell saw that the balloon was dangerously swollen. He warned Gypson to pull the valve rope, but it was too late. The balloon burst and began falling fast.

With the last of the hydrogen pouring from the torn fabric, they plummeted right through bits of smoldering paper and burning fireworks cases.

But they were luckier than Sophie Blanchard. The balloon didn't catch fire. And as John Wise demonstrated around the same time, a burst balloon tends to form a natural parachute within the netting. After falling a mile in two minutes, Gypson and Coxwell landed hard, but unhurt.

The next week they took up the same balloon . . . with twice as many fireworks.

Coxwell toured Britain and Europe, flying at fairs, celebrations, pleasure gardens—anywhere they would pay him. In August 1861, he was pressured into taking up two passengers on a windy day. When they came down, they crashed through several of the stone fences that line the English countryside.

Local people found the men bloodied and covered with stones. All three were seriously injured. Doctors told the forty-two-year-old Coxwell that his flying career was over. He would be lame for life.

Coxwell refused to believe them. By Christmas he smashed his crutches and forced himself to walk without them. By spring he was no longer lame.

And then he heard that a certain scientist was looking for him.

THE SCIENTIST

JAMES GLAISHER was a man of science. He looked, thought, and talked just like you'd imagine a scientist would—if you were living in nineteenth-century England. With bushy gray side-whiskers framing his face, he seemed wise and serious. He believed in the power of careful observation; he collected scientific instruments for that purpose. When he spoke, he did so with precision.

But although he was curious about everything, he wasn't much interested in adventure for its own sake.

Once, as a young man, he lived at a scientific post on a mountain in Ireland. He spent weeks at a time in dense fog—enough to drive even an Englishman crazy. But Glaisher remembered it as the time when he first became curious about cloud formation.

His interest in the study of weather grew. In 1840 he founded the meteorology (weather) department at Greenwich Observatory. Other scientists named him a Fellow of the prestigious Royal Society.

And he began to think about using balloons in his research. Though he'd never been in one, he thought it was a shame that so few people saw them as anything more than a source of adventure and amusement.

Glaisher and a group of scientists decided to explore the upper atmosphere through a series of high-altitude balloon flights. They hired aeronauts to take their equipment aloft, but were disappointed. Nobody could go high enough.

That's when someone told Glaisher about Coxwell.

AN UNEXPECTED PARTNERSHIP

COXWELL WENT TO MEET THE SCIENTISTS in the town of Wolverhampton. They wanted somebody who could take scientific instruments at least five miles high—about 26,000 feet above sea level. (One mile equals 5,280 feet.)

Coxwell was astonished. In nearly four hundred flights, he'd never gone anywhere near that altitude. But what really surprised him was that these solid men of science hadn't done the math. Hydrogen had a known lift and a known rate of expansion as it rose. In Coxwell's words, they "might have known by ten minutes' figuring" that they needed a bigger balloon than any that existed in Britain at the time.

The scientists were no doubt surprised to be lectured by a showman. And when Coxwell described the size of balloon they'd need, they told him they couldn't afford it.

Then Coxwell did something that astonished them. He offered to build the balloon at his own expense. He promised that it would be the largest balloon Britain had ever seen. He would have it ready by midsummer. The scientists gladly agreed.

But Coxwell had a problem. After his accident, his wife had been glad to know that he would never fly again. Now, he was going to fly higher than he'd ever gone before (and at great personal expense). And she would read about it in the newspaper before he got home.

Luck was with him. He arrived home to learn that friends had already talked Mrs. Coxwell into supporting the project. It was for science, they said.

Now Coxwell knew he could keep his promise to the scientists. His wife may not have liked balloons, but she was good at building them. He couldn't do this without her help.

Soon, Glaisher arrived to find the Coxwells running a makeshift balloon factory. An empty schoolroom held hundreds of yards of oiled cloth hanging to dry. At home, the garden was full of large tents where Mrs. Coxwell supervised the workers. She served coffee every morning at four o'clock. After that, the day's balloon-making began.

Glaisher knew little about balloons, but he was eager to learn. He'd made up his mind. He was going up in the balloon, too.

THE BALLOON *MAMMOTH*

WHEN COMPLETE, the balloon later known as the *Mammoth* stood eighty-five feet tall and held more than 93,000 cubic feet of hydrogen.

Piloting this giant, Coxwell would be too busy to gather data. That's why Glaisher chose to ride along. He wanted to record the air temperature and humidity, wind speed and direction, the earth's magnetism, the air's oxygen content and electrical condition, the presence of water above, below, and inside clouds . . . and many other things to be noted at every elevation.

Glaisher knew he'd have to work quickly, so he built a little table and attached all his instruments to it. One of these was called an aneroid barometer.

It looked like a pocket watch, but inside it had a little metal box with most of the air pumped out ("aneroid" means "without air"). It showed changes in atmospheric pressure. High pressure squeezed the box's cover in; low pressure caused it to bulge out. It was connected to springs that moved the needle on the dial.

Barometers are mostly used to predict changes in the weather. For example, low pressure (indicated by a falling barometer) usually means a storm or wet weather is coming. But because the atmosphere grows steadily less dense the higher you go, a barometer can also measure altitude. Glaisher would keep a close eye on his throughout the flight.

Coxwell was happy to have a respected scientist as a partner. The aeronaut took balloons seriously and was eager to demonstrate their usefulness.

But he wondered about Glaisher. He seemed eager enough, but he'd never actually flown in a balloon. Coxwell had heard many stories of scientific men who became terrified the moment they left the ground.

Coxwell didn't dare tell his new partner of his goal: "I had made up my mind to eventually surpass all previous flights to high altitudes," he wrote. Such a flight "would sorely test our lungs and our hearts," but would "leave a mark which could not easily be surpassed."

FIRST FLIGHT

THEY SET OUT FROM WOLVERHAMPTON ON JULY 17, 1862. Glaisher kept busy as they rose, calm and precise as always. He began noting physical changes he could feel in himself. By 19,400 feet, his heart was pounding and the ticking of his watch seemed strangely loud. His hands and lips turned a dark bluish color, but not his face. He found it difficult to read his instruments. By 21,700 feet, he began to feel seasick, though the basket was steady.

This all fascinated him greatly. He wrote down everything in his notebook.

Coxwell, meanwhile, was observing Glaisher. The scientist seemed to be enjoying himself. Coxwell was pleased.

Glaisher was more than pleased. He was astounded by the world above the clouds.

When launching a balloon, it was important not only to get everyone aboard, but also to load the basket with sandbags for ballast, as shown in these sketches of French aeronauts Albert and Gaston Tissandier

"We seem to be citizens of the sky," he wrote, "separated from the earth by a barrier which seems impassable . . . We can suppose the laws of gravitation are for a time suspended, and in the upper world, to which we seem now to belong, the silence and quiet are so intense that peace and calm seem to reign alone."

They reached 22,357 feet before they could go no higher. They were well short of five miles high. (And if Silas Brooks was right, they were not quite at the altitude reached by the Harvey children four years earlier.)

Coming down, the balloon became heavy with dew from the thick clouds through which they passed. They landed hard, breaking nearly all of Glaisher's instruments.

Coxwell felt bad. He was afraid Glaisher wouldn't want to fly with him anymore. But Glaisher's only regret was that the broken instruments would delay the second flight. He couldn't wait to get back in the air again.

They made a few more flights, once going as high as 24,000 feet. Then, on September 5, 1862, Coxwell ordered an especially pure batch of hydrogen. It was time to see just how high they could go.

INTO THE DEATH ZONE

THEY LAUNCHED AT 1:03 P.M.—Glaisher wrote the time in his notebook. Rising quickly, through a gray mist at first, they burst into full sunlight at 1:17.

The miles fell away quickly: two miles high at 1:22; three miles at 1:28; four miles at 1:40. The air grew cold. The sky turned a deeper shade of blue. The faraway earth was visible only through a few patches in the clouds.

They reached five miles (26,400 feet) at 1:50 p.m. Coxwell was breathing hard. Glaisher found it hard to read his instruments and asked Coxwell to help him. They were rising fast, and the temperature was bitterly cold and falling . . . minus two degrees Fahrenheit . . . minus five.

Today, mountaineers refer to anything above 26,000 feet as the "death zone" because of the scarcity of oxygen. People can, and do, scale such heights (though usually with supplemental oxygen). But the effects of high altitude were still poorly understood in Coxwell and Glaisher's time. It was part of what they'd come here to learn.

Coxwell saw a problem. The valve line was tangled in the balloon's neck. This was common, because a balloon tends to slowly spin on its axis (like the earth itself). But if the line gets stuck, there's no way to open the valve to come down.

Coxwell knew he must act at once. He climbed up from the basket to the ring—the big hoop to which both balloon and basket were tied. Below, Glaisher peered at the barometer at 1:54. He strained to read its blurry face. The atmospheric pressure indicated that they had passed 29,000 feet—higher even than the peak of Mount Everest, the world's tallest mountain.

And they were rising at a thousand feet per minute.

One of Glaisher's arms rested on the little instrument table. He tried to move it, but it lay there as if it wasn't even part of him. He couldn't move his other arm either.

Puzzled, he shook himself, "but I seemed to have no limbs." When he turned to look at the barometer, his head flopped over onto his left shoulder.

He shook himself again. This time, his head flopped over onto his right shoulder. He fell backward, limp as a rag doll. His head rested on the edge of the basket.

He couldn't move, couldn't speak. Dimly, he saw Coxwell high above him, perched on the ring. Then everything went black.

But inside his head, Glaisher was still awake, still observing his reactions as if he were his own subject in an experiment—except that now he was frightened.

He was dying. There was nothing he could do. His only hope was that his friend could fix the valve rope and bring the balloon down quickly.

Then, as if someone had flipped a switch, Glaisher's mind shut off and his thoughts ceased.

ANGUISH

HIGH ABOVE THE BASKET, Coxwell knew he was in trouble. He had taken off his thick gloves so he could work more easily. Now, with one touch to the metal ring, his hands were frostbitten and as useless as blocks of wood.

He looked at the balloon neck, which was coated with frost. He was panting for air, making little white clouds every time he exhaled. Somehow he freed the valve rope so that it dangled into the basket. Then, resting his weight on his arms, he dropped down from the ring.

On his feet again, Coxwell noticed three things. One was the aneroid barometer. He didn't read the number the needle pointed to, but he saw that it pointed in a straight line with one of the suspension ropes behind it. He would remember that for later.

The second thing he noticed was Glaisher, passed out. Was he even alive?

The third thing he noticed was his own consciousness. It was slipping away.

The valve rope! He had to pull it before he fainted. But how? His hands were useless.

Though his brain was fading from lack of oxygen, he had an idea. Tilting his head, he grabbed the rope with his teeth. He dipped his head once, twice, maybe three times.

The balloon started down. Now only time would tell whether he'd acted quickly enough to save his friend.

With his hands frozen and Glaisher unconscious, Henry Coxwell pulled the valve rope with his teeth so the balloon could come down. They were higher than the top of Mount Everest . . . and rising

As they traveled downward and Glaisher still didn't awaken, Coxwell said he "felt an amount of anguish which can be better imagined than described."

THE DELICIOUS ATMOSPHERE

Through the blackness, Glaisher heard a voice calling. He knew it was Coxwell, but he couldn't move or speak. He felt himself being shaken.

"Do try!" Coxwell said. "Now *do*!"

Suddenly, Glaisher sat up with a gasp. He saw his instruments, then his friend Coxwell.

"I have been insensible," he said.

"You have," said Coxwell, "and I too, very nearly."

Coxwell struggled to contain his emotions. He was an Englishman of the nineteenth century. It would not do to burst into tears at such a moment.

We now know that even at 10,000 feet, the brain has 10 percent less oxygen than at sea level. You begin not to think as clearly. At 18,000 feet, oxygen is reduced by 30 percent; you can become unconscious in half an hour. The thin air at 30,000 feet can knock you out in less than a minute.

Within limits and with practice, the body can adapt. Mountain towns exist as high as 16,000 feet. Even Coxwell and Glaisher's previous flights helped acclimate them to high altitudes.

After rubbing Coxwell's frozen hands with brandy, Glaisher picked up his pencil and resumed his observations. It was 2:07 p.m. He was curious to see how high they had gone during the thirteen-minute gap in his records.

Everything pointed to the same result. He looked at the "minimum thermometer," which showed the coldest temperature of the trip (−11.9°F). He estimated how much higher they must have gone to reach that temperature. He also did calculations based on his recorded altitudes and rates of

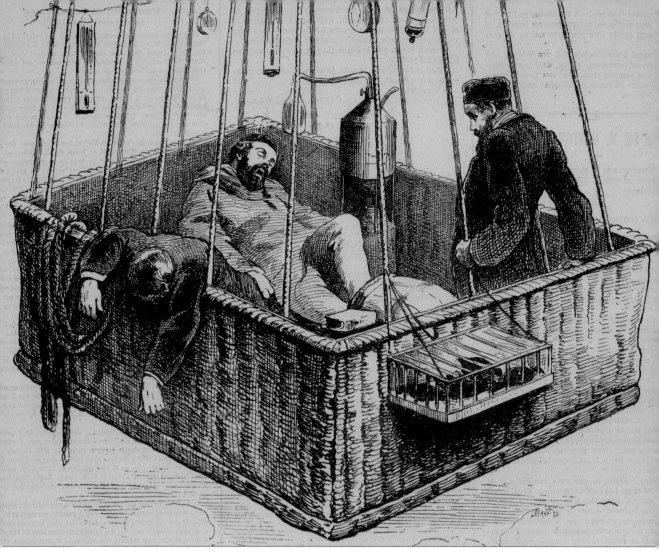

Like Coxwell and Glaisher's balloon, the French balloon Zenith *carried instruments to measure atmospheric variables such as temperature, pressure, and humidity, and had pigeons to release at high altitude. The* Zenith *also carried an oxygen-breathing apparatus (shown sitting in the basket). Even so, two of these men died during an 1875 high-altitude flight above Paris*

climb and descent. And Coxwell showed him how the barometer needle had lined up with a certain rope.

Each time, he came up with 36,000 to 37,000 feet . . . seven miles high.

And they had lived to tell about it. "How sweet and life-giving was the delicious atmosphere as we came near the ground!" Coxwell wrote.

They landed safely in the countryside at 2:50 p.m. Coxwell guarded the balloon while Glaisher walked seven miles to town to get help. He felt fine.

WONDERS THAT ARE FACTS

"We have just heard of an ascent such as the world has never heard of or dreamed of," reported the *Times* of London a few days later. "Two men have been nearer by some miles to the moon and stars than all the race of men before them."

Other aeronauts doubted the balloon soared quite as high as Glaisher thought. But no one doubted that it passed 30,000 feet. That was higher than anyone had gone before (and up where passenger jetliners cruise today).

"It is true these gentlemen have not brought down a very comfortable or inspiring report of the upper world," the *Times* continued. "Science and poetry are unhappily rather at variance upon the subject of the air and sky."

Not everyone agreed. A poem, said to be written by a schoolboy, soon appeared in the humor magazine *Punch*. It compared the flight to the legend of Icarus, the youth whose waxen wings melted when he flew too near the sun:

> Aloft 'tis cold instead of hot;
>   Wax wings would freeze, not run,
> By which a chap as near had got,
>   As could be, to the Sun.

The legend, the poet went on to say, was outdone by the real-life adventure. The closing lines ask:

Then what's the use to read about
    Old heroes' fabled acts,
When now they're beaten out,
    By wonders that are facts?

Coxwell and Glaisher had many other adventures together. But they never tried to duplicate their famous flight. Both lived to be old men.

In 1875, the French balloon *Zenith* tried to beat their record. Though it apparently rose no higher than 28,000 feet, two of the three men on board died during the flight.

By 1901, when two German balloonists soared to 35,500 feet, they breathed from newfangled oxygen cylinders. Manned balloons have since gone above 100,000 feet. But high-altitude balloonists never again tried to fly without oxygen, as Coxwell and Glaisher did. Their 1862 feat stands unmatched.

Coxwell would be happy about that. But Glaisher would take more pleasure in knowing how his research spurred future scientists to investigate the sky, using tools and methods he could only dream of.

Inside the French fort "Bastion no. 95" during the Siege of Paris in 1870. The German army had the city surrounded, and balloons were the only way out

THE SIEGE OF PARIS

The Balloon-and-Pigeon Post (France, 1870–71)

GERMAN SOLDIERS OPENED FIRE on the two French balloons floating over-head in the November sky.

"At eight hundred meters' height, the balls whistled around us," re-called a photographer named Prudent René-Patrice Dagron.

He wasn't there to take pictures. France and Germany were at war, and Dagron was traveling from Paris on a secret mission. Both balloons carried his special equipment, which he was taking to French forces in the south-ern part of the country. With Paris surrounded, this was his only hope of escape.

Just outside the city, enemy soldiers shot down and captured the other balloon. Dagron and his companions looked on with terror. They had to get away quickly.

They tried to throw out ballast, but the sandbags fell apart when lifted. Through the clatter of gunfire, they scooped up loose sand and tossed it overboard as quickly as they could.

They rose high above the earth, but they'd have to come down some-time. What if German soldiers found them when they did?

That evening, one of Dagron's carrier pigeons arrived in Paris with a hasty message from an eyewitness. It said Dagron's balloon had been shot down and captured a hundred miles east of the city.

French leaders were heartbroken. Dagron and his new technology had been a source of hope. Now he was surely on his way to a German prison . . . if he was still alive at all.

In fact, Dagron's balloon was in German hands, but Dagron himself wasn't. He had become a fugitive in his own land.

THE WAR

AS WITH MOST WARS, it's hard to state simply what the Franco-German War was about. When it began in 1870, Germany wasn't even a single country. It was a group of kingdoms led by Prussia. Prussia's prime minister, Otto von Bismarck, wanted a war with France to help him unify Germany into an empire.

In France, Emperor Napoleon III wanted a war with the Prussians to protect his own empire. He hoped a victory would restore his fading popularity with his people.

Of course, neither man explained it that way. Both countries said they went to war because the other country threatened them.

Napoleon III declared war in July. He lost a series of battles and surrendered on September 1. But the French kept fighting. They overthrew the emperor's government and declared France a republic. Meanwhile, the German army kept advancing toward Paris. The new French government fled to Tours, about 130 miles southwest of the capital.

The Siege of Paris began on September 19. For Dagron and every other Parisian, it was a day of terror and confusion. Cannon still thundered in the distance when French soldiers began rushing into the city. Many had thrown down their weapons. Dressed in braided blue jackets and baggy red pants, some were downcast, others angry. Some stormed into wine shops and got drunk.

"We are betrayed!" they said to anyone who would listen.

Angry officers shouted orders in vain. The soldiers ignored them or responded with jeers. Ambulance wagons full of wounded soldiers rumbled over the pavement. Riderless horses wandered among fleeing crowds.

In the open-air cafés along the boulevards, talk was wild with rumors. People spoke of French forces being massacred by an enemy with five times their numbers. The stories grew bigger and bloodier.

Meanwhile, the Germans cut telegraph wires and stopped all trains from entering or leaving the city. Bridges were blown up and the Seine River was guarded.

But no German soldiers appeared in the streets. After the initial panic, the French regrouped and manned the ramparts and gun platforms around the city's perimeter. They stacked sandbags and planted rows of sharp metal spikes into massive earthworks. Never before had an army surrounded so large a city, but Paris and her two million residents meant to fight.

Nearly half a million French soldiers and militiamen camped in the city's great public gardens. It was a strange sight: horses picketed under trees; cannon and ammunition wagons parked on terraced walks; soldiers huddled around campfires among fountains, flowerbeds, and marble statues.

By day, new recruits paraded in the streets. By night, the city grew eerily quiet. Wind whistled through the tents and barricades. Patrols tramped through the streets with a measured tread.

"Qui vive?" a guard would challenge a passerby. ("Who goes there?") And woe to the person who didn't have a good answer. People imagined enemy spies lurking everywhere. Foreigners were particularly suspect, but just about anyone could find themselves accused of treason. Mobs rounded up strangers and beat them senseless, or hauled them off to jail to be beaten by patriotic drunkards and criminals.

Lacking news from the outside world, Paris newspapers helped spread

One of the Paris balloons descends over the Seine River during the siege

the fear. One paper printed a rumor that the city's blind beggars were spies. Another noted that the city's English were also suspect, and suggested shooting them all, just in case.

To fight the war (and to keep its sanity), Paris needed to communicate with the outside. But there was no escape by land or water. Only the sky remained free.

BALLOON FACTORIES

A FEW BRAVE PARISIANS tried to smuggle messages hidden in hollow coins or coat buttons, even sewn up beneath their skin. Some got through, but not enough.

The city's aeronauts convinced the post office that balloons were the answer. On September 23, an aeronaut named Jules Duruof took off in an old balloon carrying more than two hundred pounds of mail. High over enemy lines, he watched through a telescope as the Germans fired cannons at him. The cannonballs rose almost straight up . . . then fell back down.

Duruof taunted the soldiers by tossing out visiting cards with his name on them. He landed safely beyond enemy-occupied territory.

Aeronauts set up balloon factories at two railway terminals, which were empty and silent without the trains running. The Godards, a husband-and-wife aeronautical team, supervised the Orléans terminal. Under an enormous iron and glass roof, long strips of freshly varnished yellow, blue, black, and green calico hung to dry from metal rafters. Visitors said they looked like banners in a cathedral. The varnish sealed the fabric so hydrogen would not pass through it. After the balloon was sewn together, more varnish would seal every needle hole in every seam.

The work took place on platforms between the rails. Teams of women cut out strips of fabric to precise measurements. Sailors made netting and built wicker baskets. From start to finish, it took twelve days to build a balloon.

With few qualified aeronauts in the city, sailors soon became balloon pilots. They made their first flights after only brief instruction. They faced death, injury, or imprisonment if they failed.

But getting messages out was only half the problem. How did one send mail *into* the city? Balloons wouldn't work. An outbound balloonist could travel in any direction, so long as he flew beyond German lines. But coming in, even a great city was too small a target for something as uncontrollable as a balloon. The French needed fliers who could navigate.

DAGRON'S SECRET TECHNOLOGY

PARIS NEEDED SOMEONE who could fly into the city like a bird. So why not use birds? Pigeons, to be exact. Pigeon racing was a popular hobby among the working classes in Europe and America. People took their birds in crates to distant locations and released them. Though no one knew how the pigeons did it, they would find their way home.

Because of their homing instinct, pigeons were also good messengers. You couldn't tell a Paris pigeon to fly a message to Tours, but if you took the pigeon to Tours, it would carry a message home to Paris.

That's exactly what the aeronauts began to do. The next balloon carried a cage of pigeons out of the city. The Pigeon Post was underway.

Carrier pigeons return home to Paris after leaving the city in balloons. During the siege, letters and pigeons went out by balloon, and pigeons carried microfilmed messages back in

But a pigeon could only carry so much. The usual method was to roll up messages and stuff them into a quill, attaching this to a central tail feather. One man used photography to shrink handwritten messages, but a better solution came from the photographer we've already met: Dagron.

Dagron grew up as a peasant in rural France. As a young man, he went to Paris to study physics and chemistry. He became involved in the new invention of photography, and struggled to make a living as a portrait photographer. On the side, he learned how to shrink images to almost microscopic size on film.

In 1859, Dagron received the world's first patent for microfilm. Most people thought it was only a novelty, but he realized that it could store large amounts of information in a very small space.

During the siege, he developed a way for one pigeon to carry thousands of messages. He printed messages on sixteen very large pages, photographed them, and then reduced them onto a single piece of film measuring two inches by one and a quarter inches. One piece of film could hold all the words in this book, with plenty of room to spare.

An early type of electric light projected the film onto a large screen, so that clerks could write the messages on paper. In a world without telephones or light bulbs (both would be invented in the 1870s), this was amazing technology.

Only one problem remained. Dagron and his special equipment were in Paris. To create microfilms for the pigeons to carry, he needed to be with the French forces outside Paris.

There was only one way to get there.

DAGRON'S ADVENTURE

DAGRON LEFT PARIS in the balloon *Niepce* on November 12. Piloted by a sailor, the balloon carried five men and more than half a ton of photographic equipment. Another balloon left at the same time with more of Dagron's gear—but as we have already seen, it was shot down just outside the city.

The *Niepce* continued on for four hours until its ballast was all but gone. The men came down fast, in case enemy soldiers were watching. They wanted to be gone before the Germans found their balloon.

They landed hard, and the wind dragged them a mile on the ground before they came to rest. By then the balloon was shredded, and everyone was tangled in the ropes.

A group of peasants came running. They told the men they were a hundred miles east of Paris, but warned that German soldiers were coming. They dressed the balloonists in peasant caps and smock coats so they would blend in, and fetched two carriages to haul away the equipment.

The soldiers came and captured the balloon and one of the carriages. The other escaped through a field. The Germans couldn't find the balloonists, though. The only people around were a bunch of "stupid peasants," who said they didn't know anything about a balloon.

When the soldiers left, Dagron and his friends drove the remaining carriage southwest toward Tours. In each town, local people gave them shelter and sent them on to someone they knew in the next town. Time and again, the men stopped someplace to rest, only to have peasants warn them that German soldiers were coming.

In one town, local people packed Dagron's equipment into empty wine casks. They told the Germans that Dagron was a teamster, and helped him get a pass to transport wine.

In another town, Dagron and his friends checked into a hotel, then found that it was filled with German soldiers. Dagron knew he couldn't leave without arousing suspicion. He ended up dining at the host's table with a group of Prussian officers. One officer offered to bet a hundred talers (a German silver coin) that Paris would fall in two weeks' time. He even handed Dagron his business card, so that Dagron would know how to contact him to settle the bet. The next step, of course, would be for Dagron to hand over one of his cards—thus revealing his identity and where he lived.

"Needless to say I did not accept," Dagron wrote.

Dagron's group left town before dawn—just before the soldiers blocked all exits.

Town to town, the adventures and narrow escapes continued. By November 18, they had to leave the road and push the carriage through a muddy field in a downpour. The field was crisscrossed with the fresh tracks of German cavalry horses. When Dagron finally reached French lines, suspicious soldiers refused to let him through.

Dagron had lost much of his equipment by the time he reached Tours on November 21. He borrowed items and improvised, and began sending microfilmed messages to Paris in early December.

At last, the Pigeon Post became a high-volume operation. Military messages and private mail began moving back and forth in great quantities. Aeronauts had dreamed of airmail for years; now the French were doing it on a scale that would not be equaled for half a century.

ROAR

BUT THE PIGEON POST'S GREATEST AERIAL ADVENTURE came just before Dagron began sending his microfilms back to Paris. By then, the Germans had introduced a new long-range cannon with a telescoping barrel. It was designed to shoot down balloons—the world's first anti-aircraft gun. Though its accuracy was greatly exaggerated, Paris authorities banned daytime balloon ascensions.

On November 24, a balloon called *La Ville d'Orléans* took off at 11:30 p.m. A sailor named Paul Rolier was the pilot. A sharpshooter named Deschamps was his passenger. They carried mail and important military messages.

A fine rain was falling in a pitch-black night—no chance the Germans would see them. Rolier couldn't see anything himself. He decided to play it safe and keep going through the night. Around three a.m., he and Deschamps began hearing a roaring sound coming from below. They guessed it was a railroad. It seemed odd, though, that they never heard a train whistle.

The sound continued as the night faded toward dawn. Above, the stars winked out one by one. Below, a light fog covered the earth. Rolier let the balloon descend slowly. The fog began to glow and burn off under the rising sun. The men could see a great blackness beneath the fog—a dense forest by the look of it.

They sank lower, and began to see flecks of white on the dark surface, like patches of snow that hadn't melted away. The forest seemed to have no end—and that strange roar kept growing louder.

At last they drew close enough to see that the patches of "snow" were disappearing and reappearing, just like . . . *wind-swept waves.*

Rolier felt a cold sweat form on his brow. The roaring sound was the ocean, and he'd been listening to it for three hours. As the fog vanished, he could see no land except a bit of coastline far to the west. But they were heading north. And sinking.

SEA AND SNOW

THEY TRIED TO DESCEND TOWARD A SHIP, but flew past it while still high in the air. An aerial novice, Rolier lacked the skill of John Steiner. By the time the balloon's guide rope was dragging in the water, Rolier realized that they had only one chance of survival: they had to stay in the air.

But the rope dragging in the sea pulled them down. The basket hit the water. The waves spilled over them. Desperately, they threw out ballast and one of their heavy mailbags.

They threw out so much weight that the balloon shot 15,000 feet into the sky. A little earlier, Rolier had tied the balloon's neck closed to keep hydrogen from escaping. Now he struggled to open it quickly, before the expanding balloon burst.

Meanwhile, Deschamps seemed to have given up. He was quiet, resigned to death. But Rolier, the sailor, was determined to keep going.

They flew on through a high, cold mist that covered everything with frost, even their hair and clothing. When the sun came out again, the balloon was covered with needles of ice that sparkled in the sunlight.

They sailed on over a heavy floor of clouds. Eight hours had passed since they'd realized they were over the ocean. They might be hundreds of miles from land by now.

The balloon was sinking again. It couldn't fly on forever. They entered a cloud that was dank with the sulfurous odor of an electrical storm. Above, they heard the crack of ice as the balloon's frozen fabric shifted.

Then they saw a black point below, something sticking up through the fog. The men got ready—Rolier on the valve rope, Deschamps holding one of the last ballast bags—in case they needed to rise quickly to avoid . . . whatever it was.

But as they drew near, the black changed to green. It was the top of a fir tree!

The men shouted with joy, and Rolier pulled the valve rope. Within minutes they struck deep snow. Rolier leaped free, but Deschamps's leg became tangled in the ropes. The balloon was carrying him away!

Rolier grabbed hold of the basket, but the balloon kept flying. At last Deschamps freed himself, and the two men let go and dropped nearly fifty feet. Only the deep snow saved them from injury.

Rolier tried to catch the guide rope, but it slipped through his cold, stiff fingers. The balloon and their gear floated away without them.

It was 2:20 p.m. After fourteen hours and forty minutes in the air, the two exhausted and hungry men collapsed on the ground. They had survived!

But when they came to, their joy turned to fear. They were alone and completely lost. They didn't even know what country they were in. They had no food or equipment. The snow, already deep, was falling in big flakes. Before them they saw a rocky, ice-covered mountain, surrounded by a forest of firs. There was no sign of humans.

Details from a French poster that proudly commemorates all sixty-six wartime balloon flights from Paris. The illustration at left shows Dagron's microfilm being projected on a screen. Rolier and Deschamps's snowy adventure is shown at right

LOST IN A STRANGE LAND

ROLIER AND DESCHAMPS HEADED SOUTH, stumbling through knee-deep snow. They saw no one except three wolves, who watched them from a distance.

After hours of hiking, Rolier's strength gave out. He sank down into the snow. Now Deschamps was the strong one. He made a bed of fir branches for his friend, and then went looking for shelter. He found an old cabin. Its roof was caved in under the snow, but it had some hay to keep them warm.

That night, as the aurora borealis (the northern lights) shimmered eerily in the sky, the two men took turns sleeping to make sure they didn't freeze to death.

They arose early the next morning, weak with hunger. Heading south again, they saw fresh wolf tracks in the snow. But soon they also saw sledge tracks and horses' hoofprints.

They came to a cabin. It was crude, with animal skins on the windows and only a hole in the roof for a chimney, but dying embers glowed in the fire pit. Someone had just been there!

Even better, the cabin was stocked with food. Famished, the men helped themselves and hoped that their hosts would be kind.

And they were. Two woodsmen soon returned to the cabin. They made coffee and brought out bacon and sausage. They chatted amiably . . . but Rolier and Deschamps couldn't understand a word. They didn't even recognize the language.

At least it wasn't German.

Rolier solved the mystery when he lit a cigarette. One of the men handed him a matchbox, which gave the manufacturer's address in the city of Christiania.

Rolier knew of that city. It was the capital of Norway!

On his first balloon flight, Rolier had piloted his ship from Paris, France, across the North Sea to Seljord, Norway—a distance of eight hundred miles (matching Wise and La Mountain's great journey of 1859). Within days, he and Deschamps were Norwegian celebrities. Their visit to Christiania (known today as Oslo) became a series of celebrations. Everyone wanted to meet the French heroes. Their balloon was found; today the basket is proudly displayed at the Norwegian Museum of Science and Technology in Oslo.

THE SIEGE ENDS

OF SIXTY-SIX BALLOONS launched from Paris during the siege, fifty-eight landed safely in friendly territory. The Germans captured six balloon crews; two disappeared without a trace. The Balloon-and-Pigeon Post delivered two and a half million letters.

But it didn't change the outcome. As the siege dragged on, food became more and more scarce in Paris. Bread rations declined, and shops began selling horsemeat, then dogs and cats.

As in all wars, the poor suffered more than the rich, and women and children suffered most of all. The soldiers were always fed first. Weakened by hunger, people fell prey to a variety of diseases, and the great number of funerals for children discouraged even the staunchest French patriot. Surrender came by the end of January.

Balloons were never again relied upon for airmail service. France and Germany were not through fighting each other, but by the time they went to war again, in 1914, the weapons were far deadlier, and balloons were no longer the only ships in the sky.

MERRICK'S AMERICAN STANDARD
SIX CORD

By the end of the nineteenth century, many Europeans and Americans were obsessed with reaching the North Pole. Swedish explorer Salomon Andrée thought it could be best done by air, an attitude reflected in a thread advertisement from the period. Unlike modern corporate sponsors, however, this company didn't pay to be the official thread of the expedition. They merely cashed in on the spirit of the times, while avoiding the mention of Andrée's name

THE NORTH POLE BALLOON

SALOMON ANDRÉE'S EXPEDITION
(SWEDEN AND THE ARCTIC OCEAN, 1897)

SALOMON ANDRÉE was growing red in the face. He stood before the International Geographic Congress in London. The auditorium was full of famous scientists and explorers. The big Swede had come to tell of his plan to fly a balloon to the North Pole, and to ask for their support.

It was not going well.

"I believe it is possible to venture further into the Arctic in a few days' balloon flight than during a century of exploration on foot," he said. Then one famous explorer after another rose to tell him why he was wrong.

One man argued that Andrée wouldn't be able to see what was below in cloudy weather, which would make the journey pointless. Another said Andrée would be lucky to make it back alive. Still another said the whole idea was "foolhardy, and not one to be seriously discussed at a meeting of this character."

Soon the auditorium echoed with mocking laughter. Andrée told them that he'd go to the North Pole whether or not they supported him.

"I do not ask for money," he said. "I have got all that I need, and the attempt will be made."

He was telling the truth. Prominent Swedes such as Alfred Nobel (the inventor of dynamite and the founder of the Nobel Prize) had already donated the money. Even the king of Sweden had donated.

Andrée had come to London not for money, but for respect. That desire had been driving him for much of his life.

YOUNG ANDRÉE

ANDRÉE HAD BEEN THE KIND OF CHILD who asks difficult questions of adults and isn't satisfied with pat answers. He liked experiments and games that involved solving a problem. His love of science led to a career in engineering.

But it was travel that revealed his true calling. In 1876, he visited America's Centennial Exposition in Philadelphia. It was full of exhibits of the latest technology. Even better, he met John Wise, who taught him about aeronautics and balloon construction, and shared his dream of riding regular air currents to distant locations.

In 1882, Andrée joined a scientific expedition to the Arctic islands of Svalbard. Some of the other scientists weren't impressed with him. One of Andrée's responsibilities was figuring out how much kerosene to bring. He didn't bring enough, and the group spent a dark winter without sufficient oil for their lamps.

Andrée wanted badly to become a famous scientist and explorer—a man whom other scientists would respect. He was so single-minded in his ambition that he never married. He feared family commitments would harm his career.

Slowly, his interest in the Arctic and his dreams of air travel began to come together. In 1893, he received a grant to buy a balloon for experimental flights. During those flights he made an important discovery—something that he believed would allow him to steer a balloon all the way to the North Pole.

A BOLD PLAN

WHY THE POLE? By the late nineteenth century, scientists and explorers were obsessed with it. The North and South Poles were considered the last undiscovered regions on earth. By the time Andrée announced his plans in 1895, generations of explorers had visited portions of the harsh and strangely beautiful lands near the top of the world. They returned home with tales of cold, starvation, and suffering.

FRAENKEL ANDRÉE STRINDBERG

In 1897, three men left a remote Arctic island in a balloon, in search of the North Pole

Some did not return at all. Many an expedition gained support by promising to look for explorers who were still missing.

Of all the obstacles guarding the North Pole, the greatest was ice. The Pole lay at the center of the frozen Arctic Ocean. Unlike a smooth frozen lake, the Arctic ice pack was rough and unstable. Ocean currents tore it apart into huge flat slabs called ice floes. The same currents would grind the floes against each other to form jagged heaps of ice called hummocks.

Sled teams crossing this tortured surface had to turn back before they ran out of food. Even ships couldn't break through, and the grinding ice could crush them into matchsticks.

So why not just fly there?

Andrée would begin his flight in Svalbard. He needed a balloon large enough to carry three men, plus ballast, plus food for four months.

The balloon would be so gas-tight that it could float for thirty days, though Andrée didn't think the journey would take that long. He spoke of Rolier and Deschamps's 1870 flight from France to Norway during the Siege of Paris. With a south wind like that, he could reach the Pole in ten hours. From there he planned to fly on toward the Bering Strait (which separates Alaska from Russia) in "not more than six days."

Still, he'd be crossing one of the harshest and most isolated places on earth, where the weather can be savage and the winds unpredictable. And success—maybe even survival—would require the longest balloon voyage ever made.

Andrée said he had found a way to do it. He would steer his balloon with sails, like the ships at sea.

HOW TO SAIL A BALLOON

While a ship can't sail directly against the wind, seamen discovered long ago how to sail *partly* against it. They learned to point their ships into the wind at an angle, with sails set at a different angle to get a push from the wind. They traveled against the wind by sailing a zigzag course, a practice known as "tacking."

Early aeronauts such as Jean-Pierre Blanchard hoped to do the same with balloons, but failed. They didn't understand that steering with sails only works on vessels moving more slowly than the wind. A ship sits in the water and the wind blows past it, but a balloon is carried along at the same speed as the wind. (That's why John Wise and his companions only knew they were in a storm by looking at the waving trees below.) If a balloon had sails, they hung limp and useless.

The trick to using sails on a balloon was to let down a long, heavy rope that trailed on the ground or water below. This would slow the balloon down enough so that the wind would blow past it and fill the sails, which could then be angled to alter the balloon's course.

Other aeronauts suggested this long before Andrée, but the Swede seems to have had more success with it than they did.

Still, his steering was limited compared to what a ship could do. Imagine a giant analog clock lying faceup on the ground. If Andrée was at the center and the wind was blowing toward 12 o'clock, he could steer his balloon for any point between 11 and 1 o'clock. Over hundreds of miles that would make a big difference. But would it be enough?

FAILURE AND DOUBT

AND SO ANDRÉE RODE A SHIP TO SVALBARD (often called Spitsbergen, the name of its largest island) in the summer of 1896. It is one of the northernmost lands on earth, lying about halfway between the Arctic Circle and the North Pole. Here the sun never sets during the brief Arctic summer. Instead, it circles the horizon day after day while the temperature hovers just above freezing.

Andrée wanted a place that was open to the north but otherwise protected from the wind. He found it on little Danes Island. Crunching through floating plates of ice, the ship entered a bay that was surrounded by barren, snow-topped mountains of black granite. On a rocky beach, the men built a four-story "balloon house" to shelter the giant balloon that Andrée named the *Eagle*.

To join him in the balloon, Andrée chose two scientists named Nils—Nils Eckholm and Nils Strindberg. They would sleep in an enclosed wicker car with three sleeping berths, or stand on the platform on top of the car. From there, a rope ladder led up to canvas storage packets that held most of their supplies. Three square sails were rigged on bamboo spars, and three 1,000-foot-long trail ropes hung from the balloon to drag on the ice.

And in case the balloon came down on the ice, it also carried a canvas boat and three sledges.

Slowly, everything began to go wrong. It was already late July by the time the balloon house was finished and the *Eagle* was filled with hydrogen. Less than a month remained before the ship would have to head south to avoid being trapped in winter ice. All they needed was a good south wind, but weeks passed while they waited in vain.

On remote Danes Island, Spitsbergen, some of the northernmost land in the world, Andrée's team built a roofless shelter to protect their balloon from the wind while it was being inflated

Meanwhile, the balloon was leaking. Eckholm warned Andrée that the *Eagle* would only fly for one, maybe two weeks.

"It is not enough," Eckholm said. "It would be mad to take off."

They never got the chance. Summer ended, the ship steamed south, and Andrée returned to Sweden in defeat. Though he insisted that he would try again next year, the public began to doubt him. Some said he was a fool or a fraud.

Worse, Eckholm resigned from the team. The newspapers reported his concerns about the balloon; some even suggested that Strindberg should likewise resign. Though the twenty-four-year-old Strindberg was also having his doubts (and was newly engaged to his sweetheart, Anna), he was angered by the suggestion.

"I will not be persuaded that I ought to desert Andrée," he wrote to a friend. "I gave my word last year, and I will keep to it now, even if the quality of the *Eagle* is not quite satisfactory."

Andrée even refused Alfred Nobel's offer to buy a new balloon. He felt betrayed by Eckholm, and refused to admit that he might be right.

Despite the bad publicity, many men volunteered to take Eckholm's place. Andrée chose a young, enthusiastic sportsman named Knut Fraenkel.

The final North Pole team was set.

SHALL WE TRY IT OR NOT?

THE NEXT SUMMER ON DANES ISLAND, Andrée again waited for a favorable wind. On July 6, a powerful storm nearly tore the balloon from its house. Then, at last, on July 11, a steady wind blew from the south.

But the weather was "squally" that day—prone to sudden storms. Andrée said he needed time to think it over.

Finally, Andrée called them all together.

"Shall we try it or not?" he said.

Fraenkel hesitated, then said yes.

"I think we ought to try it," Strindberg added. He had been writing a letter to Anna.

Andrée said nothing. Later, Strindberg heard him say to another man, "My companions insist on starting, and as I have no absolutely valid reasons against it I shall agree to it, although with reluctance."

It was a strange thing to say, but at least they now knew his decision. The three men climbed aboard. Strindberg asked a man on the ground to give his love to Anna, and Andrée gave the order to "Cut away everywhere!"

The *Eagle* rose over the harbor, then began sinking. As the men quickly threw out ballast, the car came down with a splash in the water, then rose again. On shore, a sailor shouted, "Look! The draglines are lying here on the shore!"

Disaster! The three heaviest trail ropes, which would allow the balloon to be steered with sails, had come unfastened. Now the *Eagle* was nothing but an ordinary free balloon, bound to follow the exact course of the wind.

The men on shore watched the balloon disappear in the northern sky. One of them wrote, "For one moment then, between two hills we can see a grey speck over the sea, very very far away. And then it finally disappears. Our friends are now shrouded in mystery."

They never saw the *Eagle* again.

Days later, a sealing ship recovered a pigeon message that Andrée sent on July 13. After two days in the air, the balloon was making "good speed," he said. "All well on board."

That was the last word from Andrée. Other messages and buoys were recovered over the next few years, but all had been sent earlier in the journey. Back home, people came to believe that the final chapter of Andrée's story would never be told.

ABOARD THE *EAGLE*

AS THE MEN ON SHORE watched the *Eagle* disappear, Andrée, Strindberg, and Fraenkel enjoyed bottles of ale while taking in the view from 1,600 feet. They joked while "relieving nature" over the side. While Spitsbergen vanished into the mist, the balloon crossed the edge of the pack ice. It looked dark blue in the sunlight, and was divided by lanes of open water.

The balloonists stand atop the Eagle's *car just before launch. The car had storage and cramped sleeping berths for the men*

The sun still shone at midnight, but the balloon entered the shadow of cloud cover and began to descend as it cooled. All "night" long they drifted slowly in a mist, often no more than fifty feet above the ice. At times they didn't move at all.

On July 12, they began drifting slowly westward. With the balloon weighed down by moisture from the fog, the car began slamming against the ice. The men threw out ballast, but could not get the *Eagle* to rise.

By the time they came to a standstill at 10 p.m., Andrée wrote, "we probably could not have stood it much longer."

They waited through another white night. They saw nothing living on the ice. The only sounds came from the flapping sails and the whining of the breeze through the basket. The wind was blowing, but they weren't moving.

It turned out that one of their ropes was caught under a block of ice. If not for that, the wind would have blown them back to Spitsbergen—but whether that was good luck or bad remained to be seen.

On July 13, the *Eagle* began drifting east–northeast . . . but the fog and drizzle returned that afternoon. That evening the men threw out 440 pounds of sand, buoys, even food. At last they rose to a good altitude . . . for a few hours. By 10:30 p.m. they began striking the ice again. The fog was dense.

By then, Andrée must have realized that it wasn't wind or storms that would doom the *Eagle*. It wasn't even the loss of the main trail ropes. It was fog. In the words of one of Andrée's contemporaries, Norwegian explorer Fridtjof Nansen, "Ugh! This infinitely tenacious Polar Sea fog! When it covers you with its mantle and hides from your eyes the blue above you and the blue around you and turns everything to a grey, wet mist, day in and day out, then there is required all the buoyancy of soul one possesses in order not to be depressed by its close embrace. There is fog and fog and nothing but fog wherever we turn our eyes . . . It lies on one's soul, it lies on one's senses, and everything becomes a greyness within a greyness."

The *Eagle* settled onto the ice at 7:30 a.m., July 14, 1897, never to rise again.

Using a sextant to measure the angle of the noonday sun, Strindberg calculated their latitude. They had failed to set a new "farthest north" record. They were some 500 miles short of the North Pole, about 300 miles from their starting point, and nearly 200 miles from the nearest land. Andrée's only consolation was that the 65-hour flight was—in duration, at least—the longest flight ever made.

Now there was nothing to do but go home. The journey over the ice would require all their "buoyancy of soul."

ACROSS THE ICE

Andrée stood on the roof of the balloon car, scanning the horizon all around. He saw nothing but ice. It had looked smooth from the air. Now he saw only a jumbled waste of broken, drifting ice, crisscrossed with leads of open water.

Travel was slow, exhausting, and dangerous. Each man hauled a sledge loaded with up to 450 pounds of food and gear. On the first day, one of the sledges slid into a pool of water and nearly sank.

They learned as they went. They began to team up and haul the sledges one at a time, then go back together to bring the next one forward. They learned to use ice floes as bridges across water.

And they realized that they could travel no more than a few miles a day—and even then, the ocean current could rob them of their progress if the ice drifted north. They could hear the ice moving all around them, grinding, crashing, or splitting with a crack like a rifle shot.

On July 25, Anna's birthday, Strindberg wrote her a letter (which he meant to deliver himself) that said, "it is strange to think that not even for your next birthday will it be possible for us to be home. And perhaps we shall have to winter here for another year more. We do not know yet." He was "tortured by the thought" of her worry and despair.

After five days of hauling heavy sledges with only a mile or two gained, they threw out hundreds of pounds of food and equipment. They enjoyed a big feast on the ice before they left the pile behind. Now and then they shot polar bears for food. That would have to get them by.

Day after day they exhausted themselves as they tried to reach a group of Russian islands called Franz Josef Land, where they knew there was a depot of food. But the drift of ice was against them. On August 4, they decided instead to make for another group of islands. By then they had still covered less distance than they had in the first four hours of the balloon flight.

On August 31, Andrée wrote, "The sun touched the horizon at midnight. The landscape on fire. The snow a sea of flame."

The polar summer was over. Now the nights would lengthen quickly, until the sun disappeared entirely by mid-October. Would they still be on the ice then? Could they survive the terrible cold of the long winter night?

They celebrated Strindberg's twenty-fifth birthday on September 4. Andrée had a surprise for him. All this time he had been carrying a locket that Anna had given him for the occasion. Inside, it had a photo of Anna and a lock of her hair. Strindberg looked at it for a long time, speechless.

By mid-September, the men were worn out and sick. They admitted to each other that they would have to winter on the ice.

Then they saw an island in the distance. Day by day, the drifting ice carried them toward it. They knew it was White Island, Svalbard's easternmost island.

But it wasn't as comforting a sight as you might think. White Island took its name from the glacier that covered it like a great, rounded shield of ice. Here, the glacier spilled over the island's edge; there, high cliffs of ice broke off into massive icebergs. When they did, the sound was like thunder.

It was such a forlorn place, in fact, that the men built an ice "hut" out on the pack ice even as they drifted around the island. They shot seals and bears for food, and bickered with one another. They rarely smiled or joked anymore, though Andrée believed they had enough food to last till spring.

And they had each other.

Three days after launch, the Eagle *refuses to fly farther. The men are alone on the Arctic Ocean pack ice, hundreds of miles from the nearest land. When their winter camp was discovered more than thirty years later, this was one of the undeveloped pictures in their camera*

"With such comrades," Andrée wrote, "one should be able to manage under . . . any circumstances."

Then, on October 2, disaster struck. With a great crash, water began pouring into the hut. The ice floe on which it was built had split.

They fled to the island. To their surprise, they found a bit of bare, rocky ground where they built a shelter of bones, driftwood, and tent fabric.

But after the first week of October, the men stopped making daily notes and diary entries. On October 17, 1897, Strindberg wrote, "home 7:05 a.m."

After that, neither he nor the others wrote another word.

DISCOVERY ON WHITE ISLAND

WHITE ISLAND is one of the most forbidding and least accessible lands on earth. Shrouded in mist, and almost always surrounded by pack ice, it was rarely visited by the sealing ships that plied Arctic waters.

But on a bright August day in 1930, the water was almost ice-free. The crew of a Norwegian ship came ashore to hunt walrus.

And there they found Andrée's camp, half buried in the snow: a canvas boat, equipment and canned food with Andrée's name stamped on it, a rude shelter, and, in a sitting position against a wall of rock, a headless human body with the letter *A* on its jacket. A diary was nearby, wrapped carefully in a sweater.

By then, Andrée had long been a legend among Arctic sailors, and the men were awestruck to find him at last. They investigated the camp to find out what had happened.

Strindberg, the only one who was buried, had clearly died first. He lay atop the frozen ground beneath a pile of stones. Anna's locket was in Andrée's pocket, as if he meant to give it back to her as a memento of her lost fiancé.

Fraenkel lay near Andrée. Some of the sailors thought they must have frozen or starved to death, but there was fuel in the stove and plenty of food in the camp. A loaded rifle lay near Andrée—the bears must have fed themselves only after the men died.

The bodies were returned to Sweden and buried with honors. But the cause of death remained a puzzle. Some medical scientists now believe that it was botulism—a type of food poisoning—from infected seal meat. Andrée and Fraenkel probably died soon after they buried Strindberg. It was a strange ending for men who had come so far and endured so much.

It was hard for Anna to hear the news after wondering for so long. She had waited thirteen years before marrying another man. When she died in 1949, she was buried with her husband—but she ordered in her will that her heart be first removed, cremated, and buried with Strindberg.

Many Swedes considered Andrée a hero. Others said he was a fool.

"Shall we be thought mad or will our example be followed?" Andrée wrote in his diary, while the *Eagle* still hovered above the ice. He seems to have known that he was writing for posterity when he added, "I cannot deny that all three of us are dominated by a feeling of pride. We think we can well face death, having done what we have done. Isn't it all, perhaps, the expression of an extremely strong sense of individuality which cannot bear the thought of living and dying like a man in the ranks, forgotten by coming generations? Is this ambition?"

Though the posters may have exaggerated their feats, both women and men performed aerial stunts. This poster was printed in Amsterdam, Netherlands, in the late nineteenth century

PARACHUTE GIRL

DOLLY SHEPHERD (UNITED KINGDOM, 1903–12)

DOLLY SHEPHERD DID NOT HAVE A TICKET TO THE CONCERT, but she had a plan. It was 1903, she was sixteen, and an American composer named John Philip Sousa was a famous musician of the day. They called him the "March King," after his favorite type of song.

Shepherd boarded a train to London and followed the crowd to the Alexandra Palace, or the "Ally Pally," as it was called. It was an entertainment center that held concerts, carnivals, horse races, and balloon ascensions.

She ducked into a staff entrance and asked if they were hiring waitresses. Maybe it was her smile and self-confidence, or maybe she just got lucky, but the manager hired her on the spot.

That was the first part of her plan. The second part was trickier: Shepherd hadn't mentioned that she'd never waited tables before.

But she wasn't afraid to take chances, and she could think on her feet. She watched the other girls and learned quickly. She noted with pleasure that she had a good view of the stage. Even better, no refreshments were served once Sousa and his orchestra began to play. Shepherd could stand and enjoy the show.

No one who knew Elizabeth "Dolly" Shepherd would be surprised that she'd do such a thing. She had always been daring—a tomboy who could match her older brother in tree climbing, drainpipe sliding, and other escapades. Once, she threw an inkwell at a teacher whom she felt had unfairly punished her brother. She was expelled and had to enroll in a private school three and a half miles from home. She walked there and back for the rest of her school days.

Now, thanks to her boldness, she was not only enjoying the concert, but getting paid for it as well. And it got even better. After the show, who should sit down at one of her tables but the great Sousa himself!

THE COWBOY AND THE BALLOONIST

AMONG SOUSA'S COMPANIONS were two men who would change Shepherd's life. One was an American who wore a cowboy hat and silver spurs. He had a mustache and goatee and shoulder-length hair. The other was a small, dapper man who spoke with a French accent. He wore the emblem of a balloon on his cap, and had a little parachute embroidered on his lapel. Even after Sousa traveled on to other cities, the two men remained regular customers, and always sat at one of Shepherd's tables.

Shepherd came to know the cowboy first. His name was Samuel Franklin Cody. Like the famous "Buffalo Bill" Cody (no relation), S. F. Cody was a Westerner turned showman. He had a stage show at a local theater in which he performed feats of riding, roping, and marksmanship, such as shooting an egg off his wife's head.

One night Cody arrived at the restaurant visibly upset. There had been a mishap at last night's show. He had grazed his wife's scalp with a bullet. She would not be performing tonight.

It isn't clear which bothered Cody more: nearly blowing his wife's brains out, or having to skip part of his show. Shepherd focused on the latter. "I'll do it for you," she said. "I'll come tonight."

And she did. She went up on stage and stood perfectly still while Cody aimed a loaded Winchester rifle at a plaster egg on her head. Her moment of fear came next, when Cody's daughter came out to blindfold her father before he took the shot.

He hadn't told Shepherd about that part.

Cody fired, shattering the egg—and not Shepherd's skull. The crowd cheered.

Shepherd's courage won the showman's respect, and that had consequences, for he was also an inventor and aeronautical enthusiast. He showed Shepherd the kites he was building—kites big enough to carry a person. He said that once he had a good enough engine, he would turn one of his kites into something the world had not yet seen: a powered airplane.

This was bold talk in 1903 (many would have said crazy talk), but later that year in America, two bicycle mechanics named Orville and Wilbur Wright accomplished that very thing. Five years later, Cody himself would build and fly Britain's first airplane.

Dolly Shepherd in her parachuting costume, 1911

Shepherd knew none of this at the time. But she was intrigued when Cody took her to Captain Auguste Gaudron's workshop. Gaudron was the Frenchman from Sousa's table at the restaurant. His workshop was full of balloons and parachutes. He told Shepherd how everything worked. Seeing her interest, he asked if she would like to make a parachute descent. She didn't have to think about it.

"Yes," she said.

And though nothing came of it at the time, Gaudron did not forget.

French balloonist Jacques Garnerin began to popularize the parachute with public demonstrations in 1797

PARACHUTES

THE PARACHUTE WASN'T NEW IN DOLLY SHEPHERD'S TIME. You'll remember from the second chapter that Jean-Pierre Blanchard used to drop dogs in parachutes from his balloon. He claimed it was his invention, but the idea was an old one. In 1483, Leonardo da Vinci proposed the parachute as a way to escape burning buildings. Elsewhere, various unconfirmed stories tell of parachute jumps many years before the balloon flights of the 1780s.

But the man who did the most to introduce the parachute to the world was a Frenchman named Jacques Garnerin. He was a student of Jacques Alexandre César Charles, the inventor of the hydrogen balloon.

Garnerin took his first balloon flight at age nineteen, and later became a balloonist for the French army. Captured by enemy soldiers, he spent two years imprisoned in a Hungarian fortress. It was there that he first started thinking seriously about parachutes. He thought about secretly making one as a means of escape. He could jump down from the tower and run away.

He never tried it—not as a prisoner, anyway. But even after his release, the idea wouldn't go away. In 1797, Garnerin created a sensation with a public demonstration in Paris.

Sailing high above the city in his balloon, he pulled a cord, and suddenly the balloon ripped open and the basket dropped away like a stone. The crowd gasped.

Then a large, umbrella-like parachute opened and sank slowly to earth, swinging wildly from side to side, while the man in the basket hung on for dear life.

Garnerin became a national hero—and made the parachute famous as well. His niece, Elisa, became a famous parachutist whose popularity rivaled that of Sophie Blanchard.

Then, in 1837, an English parachutist plunged to his death before a large crowd. The accident confirmed what a lot of people had been thinking—that while ballooning might be dangerous, parachuting was nearly suicidal.

Half a century passed before a new generation of parachutists appeared. By then, balloon ascensions weren't drawing the crowds they once had. People wanted something more. Starting in the 1870s, aerial acrobats began dangling from trapeze bars, performing stunts, or shooting off fireworks. An American woman known as Leona Dare even hung from her balloon's trapeze bar by her teeth.

A balloon launch in Broken Bow, Nebraska, in 1903. Though Dolly Shepherd preferred hydrogen balloons, she often parachuted from "smokies" like this one, which were inflated over a fire pit

To avoid the expense and slow inflation of gas balloons, showmen began using crude "smoke balloons" that inflated in minutes when held open over a bonfire. Such balloons had no valves and no ballast. Once they were airborne, there was no way to control them. They shot quickly into the sky, and came down fast as they cooled off.

"Smokies" and acrobats made ballooning exciting again. But much of the excitement came from knowing that the day's festivities might end with a crowd gathered around the broken body of some young woman or man who had just fallen to a gruesome death.

Then, in 1887, an American balloonist named T. S. Baldwin topped everyone by adding parachute jumps to his show. The following year he drew crowds of 30,000 to 50,000 people at London's Alexandra Palace.

Soon a new generation of young parachutists took to the sky to thrill the public.

But a year after arriving at the Ally Pally for the Sousa concert, Dolly Shepherd had no idea that she was about to become one of them.

GO!

AFTER HEARING NOTHING FOR A YEAR, Shepherd was surprised when Captain Gaudron asked her if she still wanted to try a parachute descent. Naturally, she said yes.

You may know about modern parachutes—how they're strapped to your back with a secure harness, how you pull the rip cord to release the chute. Put that out of your mind. That kind of parachute didn't exist in 1904.

When Shepherd arrived at Gaudron's workshop, he first asked her to squeeze his hands as hard as she could. Then he told her to hang from a trapeze bar.

With both hands on the bar, Shepherd hung there feeling silly. Gaudron, however, nodded with satisfaction. The girl had strong arms and a firm grip. She would need both.

On the day of her first jump, Shepherd arrived at the Ally Pally and changed into her new uniform, a navy blue suit with loose-fitting trousers, gold trim, a gold sash around her waist, and a high-peaked cap. Like Captain Gaudron, she had a balloon emblem on her cap and a little parachute on her lapel. In all, she thought it was "very swish." In an age when women always wore long dresses, this was a daring costume. Heads turned as Shepherd walked through the crowd toward the balloon.

Shepherd climbed into the balloon basket with the captain and four passengers. Not only was it her first parachute jump, but it was also her first balloon ride. She watched with wonder as the balloon rose and the cheering faces on the ground fell away. In her mind she rehearsed what

Gaudron had told her during her half hour of training. Then suddenly he said, "We are over two thousand feet. Get ready to jump."

To Shepherd, perched on the edge of the balloon basket with her legs dangling over the side, the words felt like "a piece of ice being dropped into the pit of my stomach."

The parachute hung limp from the balloon netting, tied to it by a single cord that would break as soon as Shepherd put her weight on it. She straddled a six-inch strip of webbing that was tied in a loop to the parachute. This sling would bear most of her weight, though she also held a trapeze bar above her head.

As her sole precaution, she also wore a safety belt that connected her to the bar. Gaudron had told her she had to use the belt for her first jump. After that it was up to her.

It was probably a good thing that Shepherd didn't yet know why Gaudron had asked her to join his team when he did. She found out later that she was the replacement for a young woman who died of her injuries after a parachuting accident.

But it probably wouldn't have made a difference even if Shepherd had known. She knew that people died doing what she was about to do. She just didn't think it would happen to her. Mostly she worried about making a fool of herself by breaking a leg and letting everyone down.

So, when the captain said, *"Go!"* she launched herself into thin air.

Then she fell . . . and fell . . .

And fell.

Whoosh! She heard the canopy open above her, felt the tug of the chute's resistance. Suddenly she was no longer falling. She was floating, light as a feather on the wind. She felt "a sense of elation such as I had never known."

She landed gently, falling over on her back as the captain had taught her.

A man with a horse and carriage came to pick her up, and soon she was back among the cheering throng at the Ally Pally.

Cheering *her*.

DANGER IN THE SKY

DOLLY SHEPHERD BECAME A REGULAR PERFORMER with Gaudron's troupe. All summer long she parachuted at fairs and local celebrations across Britain. She learned to fly solo, going up without a basket beneath a small smoke or gas balloon. She preferred gas balloons because they could go higher, and Shepherd always liked to go as high as possible before pulling the cord that released her chute from the balloon.

Before each performance, she walked among the crowd, shaking hands and chatting with people. Everyone wanted to meet her. Something about being a young woman who was about to face the possibility of death made her more than a celebrity. She listened as people told her their troubles and life stories. And when it was time to launch her balloon, the crowd saw her not just as an entertainer, but as a friend.

As the crowd cheered, she rose swiftly into the sky, holding the trapeze bar with one hand and waving a small Union Jack with the other. Looking down at the distant earth between her boots, she felt like she was walking on air.

But the danger was real. Even though the others said little about it, most probably shared Shepherd's attitude: "It might happen to *them* but never to *me*." In 1906, the British government considered banning dangerous performances by women (it apparently didn't bother people as much when men got killed). But the shows went on, and year after year, Shepherd kept coming back.

Now and then she had close calls. She landed on a steep rooftop and only avoided a Sophie Blanchard–style death by clinging to the chimney pot. She once came so close to being hit by a train that her feet skimmed the roof of a car passing beneath her. She survived a wild flight through a thunderstorm. Another time, her parachute failed to open and she plummeted nearly a mile straight down. The chute finally opened just before she hit the ground. Though badly bruised, she wasn't seriously hurt.

One evening when her release cord jammed, she found herself a prisoner of her hydrogen balloon. Singing to herself as the hours passed, she shivered as the balloon rose higher and higher. Before the daylight faded, the aneroid barometer she wore like a wristwatch told her she was at 12,000 feet and rising. Her hands—held all the while on the trapeze bar above her head—were growing numb.

She hung on into the night, sailing by moonlight above the clouds. At last her balloon settled to earth, three hours and thirty-five miles from her starting point. Shepherd lay exhausted in a pasture until some horses found her and nuzzled her back to awareness.

But her greatest adventure was still to come.

RESCUE AT 11,000 FEET

Through all this, Shepherd's father was the only family member to watch her perform. Everyone else was too worried for her safety. Even her many admirers mostly said they'd never try anything so foolish themselves. But in 1908 a friend begged Shepherd for a chance to try parachuting.

Her name was Louie May, and she was engaged to be married. Shepherd arranged a meeting with Captain Gaudron and did her best to make sure that Louie's fiancé didn't find out.

The two women would make a double descent—two parachutes attached to the same basketless balloon, about eight feet apart.

The ascent went perfectly.

"I wouldn't have missed this for *anything*!" May said.

At 3,000 feet, Shepherd said it was time to drop. May pulled her release cord . . . and nothing happened. The balloon kept rising.

May was stuck, just as Shepherd had once been stuck. During that long night, Shepherd had held on for more than three hours. But could May last that long?

They passed through the clouds at 8,000 feet. Shepherd could see that her friend was becoming terrified. By 11,000 feet, May's face was pale and her lips were blue with cold.

Shepherd could pull away and save herself, but doing so would send May soaring to even deadlier heights. No. She had to stay, and she had to think of something fast.

She could see only one chance. They would have to come down on the same parachute.

Grabbing hold of a cord, Shepherd pulled May's trapeze bar toward her until the two women were face-to-face. Then, step by step, she instructed May to climb out of her own sling and wrap her arms and legs around Shepherd.

May obeyed, knowing that with one slip she would punch a hole in the clouds on a two-mile plummet to certain death. Shepherd wondered if her arms—and the chute itself—could bear the added weight the whole way down.

Dolly Shepherd ascends from the Pickering Gala in 1911. Other than having one foot in a sling, she was simply holding on to a trapeze bar. Her parachute was suspended from the balloon; when she flew high enough (and she liked to fly high), she would release it and float back to the ground

With a tug on the release cord, they dropped.

They entered the darkness of the clouds, then burst out into the light below. The ground was coming up fast. Too fast. The chute had not opened all the way!

Shepherd felt a second tug as the chute opened fully, but they still landed hard, May on top.

And then they burst out laughing. They had done it! May stood up, unhurt. Shepherd lay on her back. She felt no pain. She felt nothing at all.

"Something was telling me to lie very still," she recalled. "Something was telling me that I was very badly hurt."

Shepherd cried when one of her doctors told her she would never walk again. Twenty-one years old, and having just made international news, she was to be transferred to a hospital for incurables.

But her local doctor held out hope. With Shepherd's permission to try an experiment, he returned with a black box containing wires, square metal plates, and a large battery. Wiring Shepherd to the battery, he fiddled with the machinery until Shepherd felt a jolt in her back. The doctor spent the next week treating her with electricity, until she was able to sit up in bed. Day by day, she learned to walk again.

And just eight weeks after her accident, she returned to parachuting.

END OF AN ERA

THE YEAR 1908 saw not only the world's first midair rescue, but also Britain's first airplane flight. The pilot and airplane-builder was Shepherd's old friend Samuel Cody, now known as the "flying cowboy." Shows like Captain Gaudron's would go on for years, but the balloon era was coming to a close. After dominating the skies for more than a century, the balloon was now bested by the faster and more controllable airplanes and airships.

For Shepherd, the balloon era ended one day in 1912. As she rose high into the silent sky, she heard a voice, clear and distinct, up where there should have been no voice.

"Don't come up again, or you'll be killed," the voice said.

She never ballooned or parachuted again.

By the time Shepherd wrote her memoirs, shortly before her death in 1983, she was the last great figure of a forgotten profession. Her book, *When the 'Chute Went Up*, describes a world so long gone that it seems almost as if Joseph Montgolfier himself had survived into the space age.

Shepherd's daughter, Molly Sedgwick, also took up parachuting—though she started later in life than her mother. After several successful jumps with Britain's Red Devils parachute team, Molly announced that she would honor her mother's memory by making a parachute jump from the same altitude as the famous midair rescue.

No doubt Molly had plenty of friends and loved ones telling her not to do it. But she reacted pretty much as her mother once had—which is to say she trusted herself and did as she pleased. In May 2004, Molly jumped out of an airplane at 13,000 feet and landed safely. She was eighty-four years old.

Her mother, no doubt, would have roared with laughter.

NOTES

INTRODUCTION

5   appearance of airships and airplanes: Rolt, *The Aeronauts*, 230.

THE BLACK MOON

7   balloon a sign of Judgment Day: Crouch, *The Eagle Aloft*, 17. Though Crouch is describing the reaction to the Montgolfier balloon launch at Annonay, the people of Gonesse probably had a similar opinion.

8   "black moon": Marion, *Wonderful Balloon Ascents*, 46; Crouch, *The Eagle Aloft*, 17.

8   Joseph Montgolfier biography: Rolt, *The Aeronauts*, 27–29.

9   origin of the word *balloon*: Bacon, *Balloons, Airships, and Flying Machines*, 17.

10   fear that people couldn't survive flight: Rolt, *The Aeronauts*, 41.

10–14   Montgolfier experiments: Rolt, *The Aeronauts*, 26–44.

11   Archimedes and buoyancy: "Archimedes' Principle," *Encyclopædia Britannica*.

13   "What? Allow two vile criminals": Marion, *Wonderful Balloon Ascents*, 62.

14–15   Rozier and d'Arlandes's flight: Marion, *Wonderful Balloon Ascents*, 65–70.

15   Charles biography: Crouch, *The Eagle Aloft*, 24; U.S. Centennial of Flight Commission, "Jacques Alexandre César Charles," www.centennialofflight.gov/essay/Dictionary/Charles/DI16.htm.

15–18   Charles's first flight: Rolt, *The Aeronauts*, 49–54.

19   death of Rozier: Marion, *Wonderful Balloon Ascents*, 181–85.

19   "They will find out the secret": Marion, *Wonderful Balloon Ascents*, 4.

QUEEN OF THE NIGHT SKY

Unless otherwise noted, this chapter is based on Schneider, "Star Balloonist of Europe"; and Fonvielle, *Adventures in the Air*, 47–48, 130, 145–56, 179–80.

22   young Jean-Pierre: Crouch, *The Eagle Aloft*, 79–80.

22   parachuting dog: Marion, *Wonderful Balloon Ascents*, 29–30.

23   "a ruthless egotist": Rolt, *The Aeronauts*, 84.

23–25   crossing the English Channel: Crouch, *The Eagle Aloft*, 72, 84–90; Bacon, *The Dominion of the Air*, 22, 26.

25   "my gallant little captain": Rolt, *The Aeronauts*, 86.

26   Sophie's background: Lynn, *Popular Science and Public Opinion*, 132; Rolt, *The Aeronauts*, 109.

26   "incomparable sensation": Marck, *Le rêve de vol*, 216.

26   Sophie unable to speak: Brown, ed., *The Literary Magazine*, 207–08.

27   Sophie makes vow, saves money: Marion, *Wonderful Balloon Ascents*, 190.

27–28   making hydrogen: Wise, *A System of Aeronautics*, 286–90.

31   night flights: Bacon, *Dominion of the Air*, 57–58.

32   "Let's go": Ireland, *France for the Last Seven Years*, 402.

32–33   Sophie's last flight: "Foreign Occurrences," 76–77; Rolt, *The Aeronauts*, 109–10; *Memoirs of Charles Mathews, Comedian*, 65 (quoting a letter from Mathews's friend John Poole, who witnessed the crash); "Norwich Duff: Journal extract on the death of La Veuve Blanchard," manuscript page images at Arbuthnot of Kittybrewster genealogy Web site, www.kittybrewster.com/images/Norwich _Duff_Journal_pages017to018.htm.

32   "*Brava!*": Marion, *Wonderful Balloon Ascents*, 189.

33   Sophie criticized: for example, Grenville Mellen, in his 1825 book, *Sad Tales and Glad Tales*, 185, "a woman in a balloon is either out of her element or too high in it."

SPLASHDOWN IN LAKE ERIE

Unless otherwise noted, this chapter is based on *Erie Observer*, June 20, 27, 1857; and Crouch, *The Eagle Aloft*, 230–32. See also National Air and Space Museum, "The Steiner Ambrotype, 1857: First Photograph of an American Aircraft," www.nasm.si.edu/research/arch/collections/steiner.cfm.

37   "And then it heaves"; "a snarling crash"; "Then you are in a wilderness": Wise, *Through the Air*, 333, 335–36.

39   fear of comet: Flammarion, *Popular Astronomy*, 483–84.

41   "The open wicker car": Bacon, *The Dominion of the Air*, 26.

42–43 Steiner's later activities: *Erie Observer*, June 30, 1859; Crouch, *The Eagle Aloft*, 281–84; National Air and Space Museum, "The Steiner Ambrotype, 1857."

THE CHILDREN ARE GONE!

Unless otherwise noted, this chapter is based on *Frank Leslie's Illustrated Newspaper*, October 23, 1858, which quotes reports from other newspapers. *Leslie's* incorrectly gives the location as Centralia, Iowa.

47–48 Ira Thurston: Wise, *Through the Air*, 483–84; Crouch, *The Eagle Aloft*, 237.

50–51 Donati's Comet: Baldwin, *With Brass and Gas*, 40.

50   "as much as twenty miles"; "I wish it would come": Baldwin, *With Brass and Gas*, 45. Baldwin includes a newspaper account that repeats the *Leslie's* report and tacks on these more melodramatic details, referring to the children as "Jenny" and "Johnny."

52–53 death of Thurston: Wise, *Through the Air*, 484; Baldwin, *With Brass and Gas*, 79. Writing years later, Wise said the body was discovered in October, but Baldwin reprints an 1859 Cleveland newspaper report announcing that the bones were discovered March 6 and identified March 9.

THE LONG VOYAGE

55–56 Wise as youth: Wise, *Through the Air*, 28–31; Douty, "The Greatest Balloon Voyage Ever Made."

55   "could speak and tell me": Wise, *Through the Air*, 27.

56–64 the *Atlantic* and its flight: Unless otherwise noted, this narrative is based on Wise, *Through the Air*, 489–519; Wise, "An Aeronautic Narrative"; and "Statement of Mr. Hyde." See also Douty, "The Greatest Balloon Voyage Ever Made."

57   dimensions of the *Atlantic*: Crouch, *The Eagle Aloft*, 248; "The Great Balloon Voyage."

57   Trans-Atlantic Balloon Company: Baldwin, *With Brass and Gas*, 142.

60   distance across Lake Ontario: Hyde said it was nearly 190 miles to the eastern shore, but based on their course the distance couldn't have been that great. According to Wise (*Through the Air*, 508), they were in sight of Rochester, New York, when they went out over Lake Ontario; on p. 510, Wise says it was 100 miles to shore. Wise had been thinking of landing in Rochester, but they were swept out over the lake before they got there.

62   "I knew, if I should climb": Baldwin, *With Brass and Gas*, 105.

65   American distance record: Crouch, *The Eagle Aloft*, 254.

65   Wise feuds with La Mountain, disappears in 1879: "Professor Wise, the Aeronaut, at Lancaster"; "General News"; Baldwin, *With Brass and Gas*, 138–47.

65   *Double Eagle II*: Stekel, "If at First You Don't Succeed."

TO THE TOP OF THE SKY

67–69   background of Coxwell and Glaisher: Bacon, *Balloons, Airships and Flying Machines*, 60–62; Rolt, *The Aeronauts*, 140, 198; Alexander, *The Conquest of the Air*, 39–40; Lee, *Dictionary of National Biography*, 76–77; Coxwell, *My Life and Balloon Experiences*, 74–90; Glaisher, *Travels in the Air*, 29; "Obituary, James Glaisher, F. R. S.," *Observatory* 26 (1903), 130.

69–78   high-altitude flights: Unless otherwise noted, this narrative is based on Coxwell, *My Life and Balloon Experiences*, 90–99, 111–13, 137–50; and Glaisher, *Travels in the Air*, 32–60, 94.

70–71   aneroid barometer: Peck, *Introductory Course of Natural Philosophy*, 135.

71   Coxwell eager to show balloons' usefulness: He had also been involved in military balloon experiments. See Bacon, *The Dominion of the Air*, 143–49.

76   oxygen at high altitude: U.S. Centennial of Flight Commission, "The Race to the Stratosphere," www.centennialofflight.gov/essay/Lighter_than_air/race_to_strato/LTA11.htm.

78   others doubt Glaisher's estimate: Rolt, *The Aeronauts*, 197; Bacon, *The Dominion of the Air*, 168; Wise, *Through the Air*, 211; Alexander, *The Conquest of the Air*, 109.

79   *Zenith* and later high-altitude flights: Rolt, *The Aeronauts*, 198–200.

79   Glaisher's research inspired other scientists: Rolt, *The Aeronauts*, 140.

THE SIEGE OF PARIS

81   "At eight hundred meters' height": Dagron, *La poste par pigeons voyageurs*, 5.

81–82   Dagron's escape from Paris: Fonvielle, *Adventures in the Air*, 247; Rolt, *The Aeronauts*, 175.

82   Franco-German War: *Encyclopædia Britannica*, s.vv. "Franco-German War," "Otto von Bismarck," "Napoleon III."

82–84   siege begins: Vizetelly, *Paris in Peril* 1: 232, 246; 2: 1–14; Vizetelly, *My Days of Adventure*, 52–79; Markheim, *Inside Paris During the Siege*, 1, 7–12, 29; Blind, "The Siege of Paris and the Air Ships."

83   "We are betrayed": Vizetelly, *My Days of Adventure*, 67.

83   *"Qui vive?"*: Vizetelly, *Paris in Peril* 2: 3.

85   balloon factories: Vizetelly, *Paris in Peril* 1: 234–46; Fonvielle, *Adventures in the Air*, 238; Rolt, *The Aeronauts*, 173; Glaisher, *Travels in the Air*, vii–viii.

85–87   Dagron's secret technology: Rolt, *The Aeronauts*, 143, 175; Vizetelly, *Paris in Peril* 1: 244–45; Southern Regional Library Facility, University of California, "The History of Microfilm: 1839 to Present," www.srlf.ucla.edu/exhibit/text/hist_page3.htm; "Balloons and Voyages in the Air," 128–29.

87–88   Dagron's adventure: Dagron, *La poste par pigeons voyageurs*, 17; Fonvielle, *Adventures in the Air*, 247; Rolt, *The Aeronauts*, 175.

89   new cannon leads to daylight flight ban: Rolt, *The Aeronauts*, 175–76; Fonvielle, *Adventures in the Air*, 248–50; Wise, *Through the Air*, 230.

89–93   Rolier and Deschamps's flight: Wise, *Through the Air*, 233–40; Tissandier, *En Ballon!*, 207–11. See also Rolt, *The Aeronauts*, 176. Rolt appears to be in error on some names and locations. He is contradicted by Tissandier, who interviewed Rolier after the flight. Wise's account (a translation of a French article) is consistent with Tissandier's.

93   balloon basket in museum: Norwegian Museum of Science and Technology, *"La Ville d'Orléans."* www.museumsnett.no/alias/HJEMMESIDE/ntm/eng/exhibitions/highlights.htm.

93   siege ends: Rolt, *The Aeronauts*, 176; Vizetelly, *My Days of Adventure*, 62–91, 173–81; Henry Labouchere, *Diary of the Besieged Resident in Paris*, 354–66; Markheim, *Inside Paris During the Siege*, 311; Vizetelly, *Paris in Peril* 2: 244–48.

THE NORTH POLE BALLOON

This chapter is largely based on *Andrée's Story* (Andrée and Strindberg), which contains the expedition journals; and Hempleman-Adams, *At the Mercy of the Winds*. All quotations are from *Andrée's Story*, except where noted. Hempleman-Adams is an English adventurer who, inspired by Andrée, successfully flew a balloon to the North Pole in 2000. Like Andrée, he departed from Danes Island, but unlike him flew solo at high altitude in a combined helium cell/hot-air balloon, and received detailed weather updates by radio.

95   "foolhardy": Hempleman-Adams, *At the Mercy of the Winds*, 46.

96   meets John Wise; receives grant for balloon: Rolt, *The Aeronauts*, 152–53.

99   description of the *Eagle*: Rolt, *The Aeronauts*, 153–54.

100   "It is not enough"; "I will not be persuaded": Hempleman-Adams, *At the Mercy of the Winds*, 82–83, 93.

102   "For one moment then": Hempleman-Adams, *At the Mercy of the Winds*, 158.

106   "White Island" is the English rendering of Kvitøya, the island's official Norwegian name.

108   botulism: There have long been many theories about why the men died. For years the most popular was trichinosis, a parasitic disease that is usually not fatal. Hempleman-Adams reprints a 2000 paper by Dr. Mark Personne of the Swedish Poisons Information Centre. Personne believes it was botulism, which results in a spreading paralysis that can kill a person in a matter of hours. That, he says, matches the campsite's evidence of quick deaths. (An autopsy could have settled the matter, but the men's bodies were cremated soon after they were taken home to Sweden.) See *At the Mercy of the Winds*, 294–303.

PARACHUTE GIRL

Unless otherwise noted, this chapter is based on Shepherd, *When the 'Chute Went Up*.

115   parachutes: *Encyclopædia Britannica*, s.v. "Parachute"; Bacon, *Dominion of the Air*, 42–46.

115–16   Garnerin and early parachutists: Fonvielle, *Adventures in the Air*, 102–05; Marion, *Wonderful Balloon Ascents*, 150; Bacon, *Dominion of the Air*, 80–86; Crouch, *The Eagle Aloft*, 506.

116   new generation of parachutists: Crouch, *The Eagle Aloft*, 465–80, 506–10.

119   considered ban on dangerous performances by women: "Dangerous 'Turns' by Women May Be Stopped in England."

123   Molly Sedgwick: "Parachutist, 83, in Tribute to Record-breaking Mum"; "Parachute Jump Raises £6K"; "Molly, 84, Takes on a Parachute Jump."

BIBLIOGRAPHY

BOOKS

Alexander, John. *The Conquest of the Air: The Romance of Aerial Navigation*. New York: A. Wessels, 1902.

Andrée, Salomon August, and Nils Strindberg. *Andrée's Story: The Complete Record of His Polar Flight, 1897*. New York: Viking, 1930.

Bacon, Gertrude. *Balloons, Airships, and Flying Machines*. New York: Dodd, Mead, 1905.

Bacon, John Mackenzie. *The Dominion of the Air: The Story of Aërial Navigation*. London: Cassell, 1902.

Baldwin, Munson. *With Brass and Gas: An Illustrated and Embellished Chronicle of Ballooning in Mid-Nineteenth Century America*. Boston: Beacon, 1967. (A collection of balloon-related news clippings from the 1850s.)

Coxwell, Henry. *My Life and Balloon Experiences*. Part 2. London: W. H. Allen, 1889.

Crouch, Tom D. *The Eagle Aloft: Two Centuries of the Balloon in America*. Washington, D.C.: Smithsonian Institution Press, 1983.

Dagron, Prudent René-Patrice. *La poste par pigeons voyageurs: Souvenir du siège de Paris*. Paris: n.d., ca 1871.

Encyclopædia Britannica. 2004. CD. s.vv. "Archimedes' Principle"; "English Channel"; "France, History of"; "Franco-German War"; "Napoleon III"; "Otto von Bismarck"; "Parachute."

Flammarion, Camille. *Popular Astronomy: A General Description of the Heavens*. Translated by J. Ellard Gore. London: Chatto & Windus, 1894.

Stekel, Peter. "If at First You Don't Succeed . . . *Double Eagle I* and *Double Eagle II*," *Balloon Life*, February 1998, 14–15. (Describes first crossing of Atlantic Ocean by balloon.)

Wise, John. "An Aeronautic Narrative," *Brooklyn Eagle*, July 6, 1859. (Flight of the *Atlantic*.)

SELECTED WEB SITES

www.centennialofflight.gov, produced by the U.S. Centennial of Flight Commission, has resources for teachers, students, and flight enthusiasts. The essays section has a "Lighter-Than-Air" subsection with several interesting articles.

http://lcweb2.loc.gov/pp/tischtml/tiscabt.html is the homepage for the Tissandier Collection at the Library of Congress Prints and Photographs Division (www.loc.gov/rr/print/catalog.html). It's a collection of hundreds of balloon-related images from the eighteenth and nineteenth centuries, including many that appear in this book. You can browse the images and read about them, and in many cases download high-resolution versions.

Google Books (http://books.google.com) is a handy source for many of the old, otherwise hard-to-find books in this bibliography. Many of them are available in full and free of charge.

www.davidbristow.com is the author's Web site. It has materials for further reading, such as a time line of early flight, and first-person narratives of more adventures by some of the aeronauts in this book.

ACKNOWLEDGMENTS

I'd like to thank the following people for helping me with this project: my wife, Danette, who has long been my first reader (and a tactful critic); Sonia Pabley and Melanie Kroupa, who were the first two professionals to set this book on the path to publication; my agent, Susie Cohen at the Gersh Agency; and at Farrar Straus Giroux Books for Young Readers, my editor, Wesley Adams, designer Jay Colvin, copy chief Karla Reganold, copy editor Selma Rayfiel, and proofreader Helen Rubinstein. Also, I thank the staff at Norfolk, Nebraska, Public Library for their patience with my endless interlibrary loan requests.

For help in obtaining images and the right to publish them, I thank Kenneth Johnson of the Library of Congress, Kate Igoe of the National Air and Space Museum (Smithsonian Institution), Linda Hein of the Nebraska State Historical Society, R. J. Dowson of the Beck Isle Museum of Rural Life, and Barbara Sokol, daughter of photographer Sydney Smith.

ILLUSTRATION CREDITS

The following images appear courtesy of the Library of Congress, Prints and Photographs Division. Unless otherwise noted, each photo's reproduction number begins "LC-DIG-ppmsca-" followed by a five-digit number listed here: front jacket (02303), back jacket (02562), p. ii (LC-DIG-ggbain-00956), p. 2 (02482), p. 4 (02561), p. 6 (02473), p. 9 (02261), p. 12 (02228), p. 15 (02562), p. 16 (02185), p. 17 (02284), p. 20 (02561), p. 24 (03478), p. 29 (02180), p. 38 (02280), p. 42 (LC-USZC4-10456), p. 44 (02312), p. 47 (LC-USZ62-42857), p. 56 (LC-USZ62-11594), p. 66 (02302), p. 72 (02312), p. 77 (02198), p. 80 (02639), p. 84 (02307), p. 86 (LC-USZC4-10774), p. 91 (LC-USZC4-10775), p. 97 (LC-USZ62-17441), p. 100 (06220), p. 103 (LC-USZ62-78117), p. 110 (LC-USZC4-10773), p. 114 (03476), p. 124 (07435). Most of these images are from the Tissandier Collection, containing approximately 975 items documenting the early history of aeronautics with an emphasis on balloon flight in France and other European countries. The Tissandier brothers, Gaston (1843–1899) and Albert (1839–1906), were both balloonists and assembled the pictures from many sources. The images of the balloon *Atlantic* on pp. 54 and 62, and of Coxwell and Glaisher on p. 75, are from John Wise, *Through the Air* (1873). The National Air and Space Museum, Smithsonian Institution, provided the images on the following pages: p. 34 (SI 2001-5358), p. 40 (SI 82-1403), p. 46 (SI 82-1405), p. 51 (SI 82-1406), p. 57 (SI 90-6523), p. 94 (Krainik Lighter-Than-Air Collection, SI-2002-585), p. 107 (SI 2008-14639). The photograph of Shepherd on p. 113 was provided by the Imperial War Museum, London, UK (photo no. Q 98454). The photograph of the smoke balloon on p. 116 was provided by the Nebraska State Historical Society (photo no. RG2608:PH738). The photograph of Shepherd at Pickering Gala (Sydney Smith, photographer) on p. 121 was provided by the Beck Isle Museum of Rural Life, Pickering, North Yorkshire, UK.